MW00355886

Making Wood Bowls

with a Router & Scroll Saw

Making Wood Bowls

with a Router & Scroll Saw

Patrick Spielman & Carl Roehl

Sterling Publishing Co., Inc.   New York

ACKNOWLEDGMENTS

We acknowledge with much gratitude the assistance of Ralph Murre, for his excellent drawings, and the effort of our typist, Julie Kiehnau.

Library of Congress Cataloging-in-Publication Data

Spielman, Patrick E.
   Making wood bowls with a router & scroll saw / Patrick Spielman &
Carl Roehl.
      p.   cm.
   Includes index.
   ISBN 0-8069-8502-X
    1. Routers (Tools) 2. Woodwork. 3. Bowls (Tableware) 4. Jig
saws. I. Roehl, Carl. II. Title.
   TT203.5.S62 1992
   674′.88—dc20   91-42464
                                     CIP

10 9 8 7 6 5 4 3 2 1

Published in 1992 by Sterling Publishing Company, Inc.
387 Park Avenue South, New York, N.Y. 10016
© 1992 by Patrick Spielman and Carl Roehl
Distributed in Canada by Sterling Publishing
℅ Canadian Manda Group, P.O. Box 920, Station U
Toronto, Ontario, Canada M8Z 5P9
Distributed in Great Britain and Europe by Cassell PLC
Villiers House, 41/47 Strand, London WC2N 5JE, England
Distributed in Australia by Capricorn Link Ltd.
P.O. Box 665, Lane Cove, NSW 2066
Manufactured in the United States of America
All rights reserved

Sterling ISBN 0-8069-8502-X

Contents

Color illustrations opposite page 32

Introduction

Most woodworkers either have the ability to turn and polish a bowl on the lathe or at least understand how the process works. This book is about an entirely different approach to the art of making bowls of wood—one that *does not* depend upon the use of a turning lathe of any kind (Illus. i-1).

In this book you will learn how to make and assemble scroll-sawn rings into an endless variety of dramatic and unusually shaped bowls (Illus. i-2 and i-3); how to make decorative bowls with ribbed and fluted or wavy side walls that undulate smoothly in and out around their circumference (Illus. i-1 and i-4); and how to make delicate oval-shaped bowls with smoothly flowing, flaired walls that appear to defy commonly understood woodworking practices.

The processes involve a combination of tasks that range from deceptively easy to somewhat challenging to the average woodworker. For example, there are optional methods of making beautiful inlays that will be revealed here! Not only are uncommon shapes and decorations possible, but typical round shapes characteristic of lathe-turned bowls are another of many possibilities. In fact, woodturners may elect to use their lathes to complete certain steps on some bowls that can actually be made round if they choose (Illus. i-5).

However, this is not a woodturning or a woodcarving book. The information contained here presents a fresh and exciting approach that allows the average do-it-yourselfer to make some truly stunning bowls. Ordinary woodshop equipment in-

Illus. i-1. Making decorative bowls with thin, wavy walls is just one of many project possibilities described in this book.

6

cluding the router, drill press, and a small scroll saw is the only basic equipment needed. You will also need some special jigs such as ball-shaped sanders, but every essential detail for making them yourself is covered step by step.

The magical part to this approach to bowl-making is that the bowl is transformed from just one flat board to a spectacular three-dimensional form. And you can make deep bowls using almost any species of wood available. You can comfortably and without guilt use normally rare and expensive woods knowing that little will be wasted. Just one small board ¾ to 1 inch thick, rather than expensive, solid thick blanks that are not even available in many species, can be used to make fairly sizeable bowls.

An overview of the entire process and

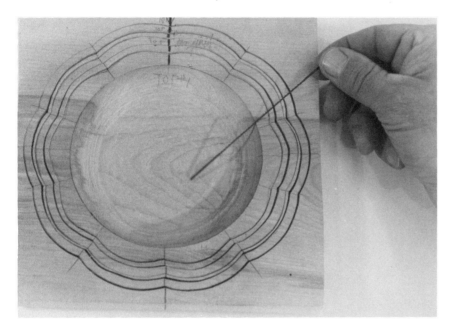

Illus. i-2. The process begins when one flat board, with a routed recess on both sides, is bevel-cut into thin walled rings with a No. 7 pinless scroll-saw blade.

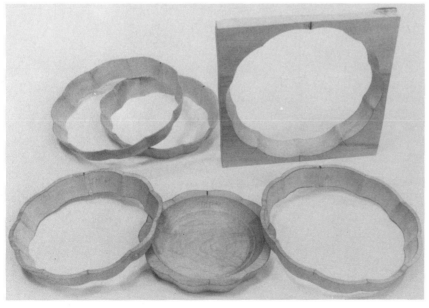

Illus. i-3. The bowl base and two rings below are glued together to form the bowl. Little wood is wasted from the initial starting blank above.

Illus. i-4. Unusual shapes, coupled with some spectacular inlay work, result in some very stunning bowls.

Illus. i-5. These bowls were not made with a lathe, but a lathe can be used, if desired, to complete bowls such as these with round shapes.

specific guidelines for your first practice bowl are given in Chapter I. Numerous full-size top-view and various optional cross-sectional plans, along with some tips on making your own designs, are presented in Chapter II. Other chapters provide detailed information about making helpful jigs, inlaying, decorating, etc. Chapter VIII deals exclusively with step-by-step procedures for making your own special sanding balls. You will find many uses in the workshop for these jigs and the other unique user-made tools and jigs detailed in this book.

The concept of stack-laminating rings cut from a single board to create a bowl is not a new one. However, the concepts involved in perfecting the process and elevating this form of bowl-making to such a high artistic level *are* new. The creation of new shapes and the revolutionary inlaying techniques explored will prove truly enlightening to the average woodworker.

All of these processes as they relate to this new form of decorative bowl-making are the brainchild of Mr. Carl Roehl, a Wisconsin woodworking artist (Illus. i-6). All of the ideas shared here are the result of almost a decade of research, trial and error, and testing. As you will note from viewing Carl's work in the following pages, he is a perfectionist and attends to every critical detail (Illus. i-7 and i-8). Together, he and I have attempted to present his knowledge and experience to the reader in an easy-to-follow, step-by-step manner so that all woodworkers can benefit from his experience.

Patrick Spielman
August 1991

Illus. i-6. Carl Roehl, a Wisconsin woodworking artist who perfected the unusual process of making decorative wood bowls explored in the following pages.

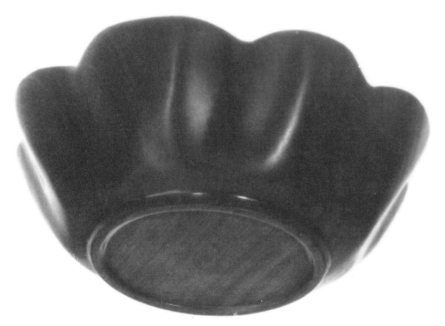

Illus. i-7. Carl Roehl devotes as much care to making a typical bowl bottom as he does to other surfaces of the bowl.

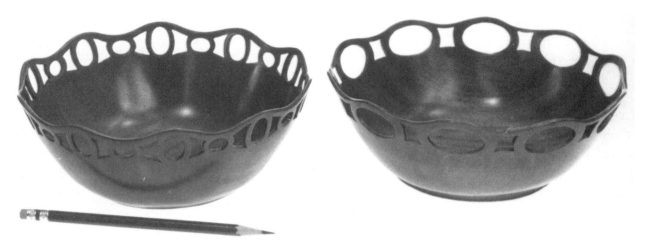

Illus. i-8. Here are just two of Carl Roehl's delicate fretted-edge bowls.

Chapter I
Basic Techniques

This chapter presents an overview of the basic stack-laminated ring procedures involved in producing a ten-fluted bowl (Illus. 1-1 and 1-2). These techniques of sawing rings from flat boards to make bowls can be applied to almost every bowl design in this book, regardless of its top-view and side-profile shapes.

Once the basic concepts and procedures are understood, they can be used with a variety of special techniques involving inlaying and other decorative practices. These decorative techniques, presented in Chapters IX–XIII, are not necessary to the fabrication of the demonstration bowl described in this chapter.

The bowl selected for a practical starting example in this chapter has an easy-to-make, ten-fluted design. It is shown in Illus. 1-1 and 1-2. A full-size pattern of a top view of this bowl is given in Illus. 1-3, along with drawings of its cross-sectional shape and an optional top-edge scallop design.

To begin making the bowl, start with a

Illus. 1-1. The basic concept for making all bowls begins with a blank, at the left, with a routed recess that becomes the bottom inside of the bowl. At the center is a blank after it has been scroll-sawn with bevel cuts to make the stacking rings. At right is the rough bowl formed by gluing the rings together.

Illus. 1-2. Left: The bowl with the rough sanding completed. Right: A completely finished ten-fluted bowl.

11

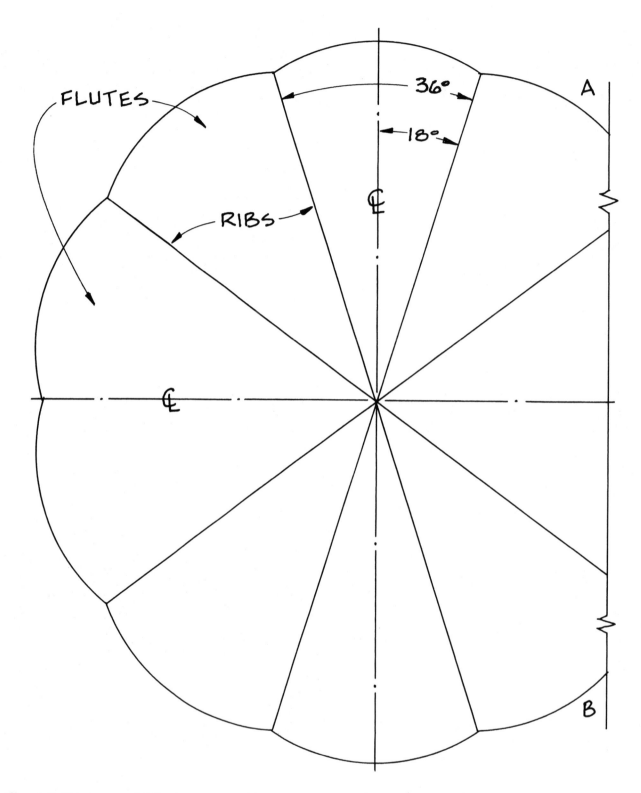

Illus. 1-3 (this page and following page). This top-view pattern of a ten-fluted bowl is all that's needed to make the bowl. The cross sections and optional pattern for the top-edge scallop are shown at the right.

12

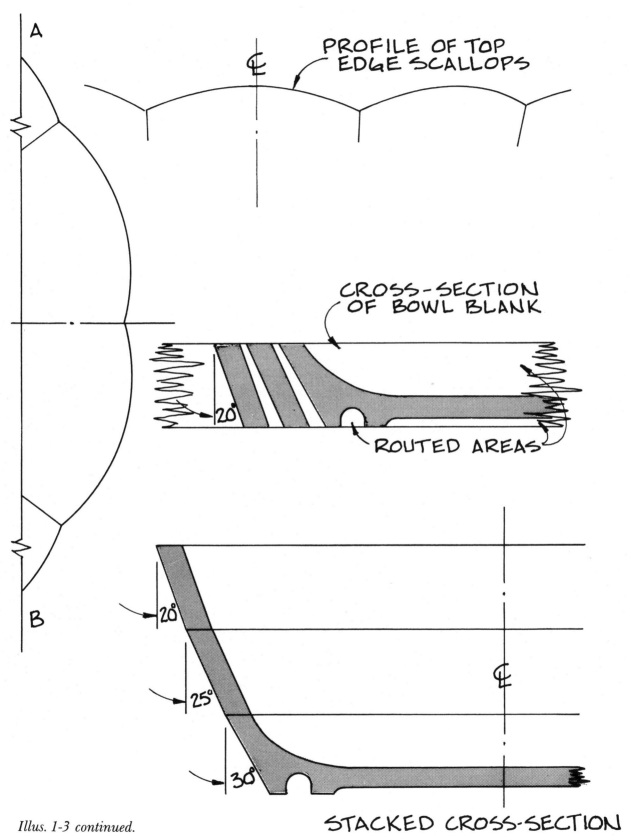

PROFILE OF TOP EDGE SCALLOPS

CROSS-SECTION OF BOWL BLANK

20°

ROUTED AREAS

20°

25°

30°

A

B

Illus. 1-3 continued.

STACKED CROSS-SECTION

single piece of wood board that's at least 7¾ inches square and ¾–1 inch thick. This piece of wood is called a bowl blank. Use a moderately priced hardwood such as birch, soft maple, walnut, or mahogany as your bowl blank for your first attempt.

It is important that you always assemble the rings and base the same way as they come sawn from the bowl blank. To accomplish this, draw register lines on both sides of the bowl blank. Use a combination square on a true edge, and draw the register lines across the center of the bowl blank on each face of the board (Illus. 1-4). Extend the lines around all the edges. Mark the word *top* on the end of one registration line on both sides of the bowl blank, as shown in Illus. 1-5.

Illus. 1-6 shows the top-view outline being drawn on the bowl blank. Note that the pat-

Illus. 1-4. Draw register lines on both sides of the bowl blank.

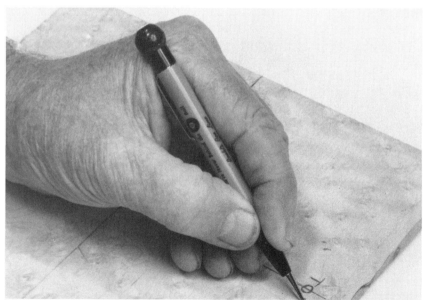

Illus. 1-5. Mark the word top *to establish a reference point for grain alignment for later assembly.*

14

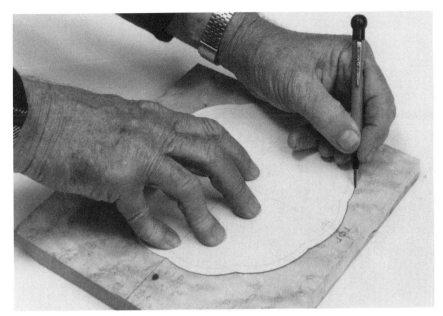

Illus. 1-7. Marking the precise locations of the ribs. It is important to be able to locate these points clearly during subsequent operations to ensure that the flutes are equal in size, and that an accurate pattern is maintained.

tern also has the registration lines that correspond to and are aligned with those on the bowl blank. Also note that the word *top* is on the pattern and is aligned with the word *top* on the bowl blank. Mark the rib locations of the flutes clearly on the bowl blank, as shown in Illus. 1-7. These lines will be extended onto the surface of the top ring after the pattern is removed.

Before cutting out the top-view outline with a scroll saw, rout the blank on its two surfaces, as shown in Illus. 1-8 and 1-9. In this preliminary routing, you will remove considerable excess material to pre-shape the bottom inside of the bowl. This is more easily accomplished now while the bowl blank still has square edges that allow for clamping during the routing process. This routing operation is explained in more detail in Chapter IV.

Begin cutting the first, or top ring. Saw the outside top-view outline with the scroll-saw table set at 20 degrees (Illus. 1-10). Next, cut the inside of the first ring. Draw a

15

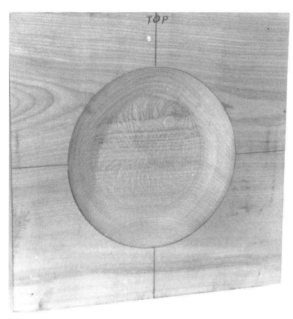

Illus. 1-8. The blank with a routed recess on its upper face. This area will become the inside bottom of the bowl.

Illus. 1-10. Bevel-sawing the outside profile with the table set at 20 degrees.

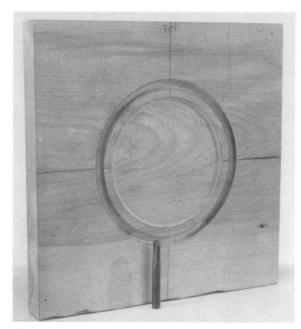

Illus. 1-9. The surface of the blank that will be the outside or very bottom of the bowl is also routed with a different recess, to create a circular ridge or "foot" on the bottom of the bowl. See the sectional drawings in Illus. 1-3.

cutting line around the outside, ¼ inch in from the edge (Illus. 1-11).

Prepare to saw the inside of the first (or top) ring. With a scratch awl, mark a point where the register line at the word *top* intersects the layout line drawn for cutting the inside of the first ring. Make the mark deep enough to drill a ¹⁄₁₆-inch hole (Illus. 1-12). Use a 20-degree-angle-supporting block to position the bowl blank, and drill a ¹⁄₁₆-inch angular hole through the bowl blank at the marked point (Illus. 1-13). For more information about making and using angle blocks, refer to Chapter V.

With the table set at 20 degrees and a #7 blade in the scroll saw, thread the blade through the hole, clamp it tight, and saw out the inside of the first ring (Illus. 1-14).

In order to maintain the grain alignment of the rings during later assembly, extend the original register lines onto the sawn surfaces of each successively sawn ring, as

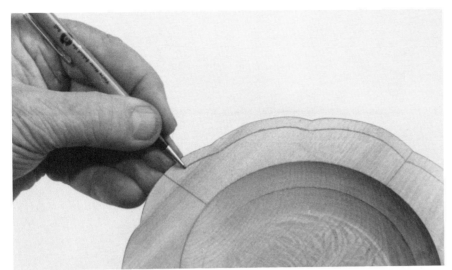

Illus. 1-11. "Finger-gauging" to lay out the cutting line for sawing the inside of the first ring. Draw a line around the perimeter that is ¼ inch in from the outside edge and parallel to it all around.

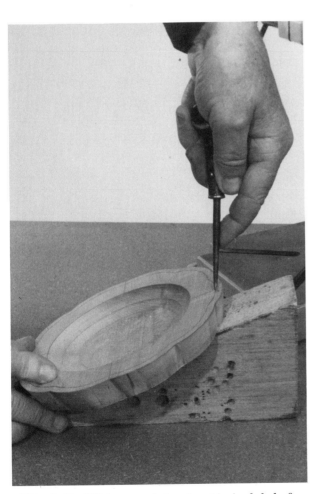

Illus. 1-12. With an awl, locate a ¹⁄₁₆-inch hole for threading the scroll-saw blade through the bowl blank. Note the use of a 20-degree angle-support block.

Illus. 1-13. Drilling a small blade-entry hole at 20 degrees.

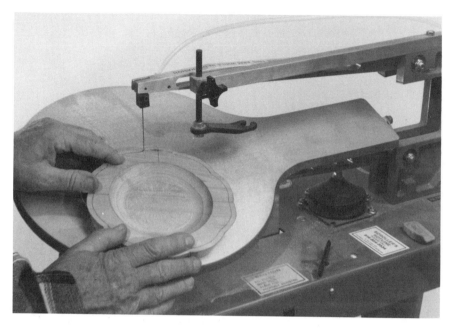

Illus. 1-14. Make the inside bevel cut of the first ring with the table at 20 degrees.

shown in Illus. 1-15. Also write the word *top* on the inside and outside sawn surfaces of all sawn rings. Then extend the marks for the ribs for the first (or actually the top) ring onto the sawn surfaces. This is done because these lines may be removed later.

Since the top of the second ring has to fit exactly to the bottom of the first ring, it is used as a pattern for marking to cut out the second ring. Make sure that the register lines and the word *top* are aligned as you trace around the inside and outside of the first ring (Illus. 1-16 and 1-17).

Illus. 1-16. The bottom surface of the first or top ring must be the same size as the top surface of the second ring. With the registration lines and the word top *all in alignment, trace the shape of the inside of the first ring to make the pattern lines used to saw out the second ring.*

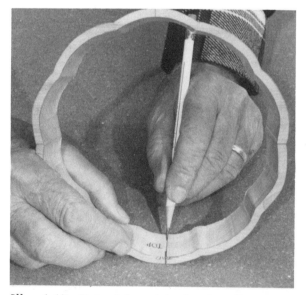

Illus. 1-15. Extend the original register lines to the inside and outside face of each ring, and mark the word top *as shown.*

18

As specified by the drawing of the cross-section in Illus. 1-3, the bowl has a curved side-view shape. This is why the second ring is cut at a 25-degree angle, rather than the 20-degree angle as before. Adjust the scroll-saw table to 25 degrees and saw the outside of the second ring. To drill for the inside cut, support the work on a combination of two angle blocks, 10 degrees and 15 degrees that are held together. (Refer to Chapter V.) Proceed to cut out the inside of the second ring.

Again, extend the register lines and the word *top* to the cut faces of this ring, just as was done for the first ring.

After the second ring is cut out, use it as a pattern for marking the outside profile of the base or bottom layer. Increase the angle of the bevel cut another 5 degrees; the final cut will be made at 30 degrees.

Illus. 1-18. All bevel-sawing of the rings has been completed. At top is the sawn waste material. The two rings and the base which will comprise the entire bowl are in the foreground.

Illus. 1-18 shows all the bevel scroll-sawing work completed. Note the two rings and the base which make up the layers for the bowl, plus the two waste rings and the outside waste material.

Illus. 1-19 shows a method of checking how well the rings fit together. If necessary, it is best to level the gluing surfaces of each layer with a special disc sander on a drill press, as shown in Illus. 1-20. This special ring-sanding disc and its operation are explained in Chapter VI. When the rings fit tightly together, without any visible gaps, they are ready to be glued.

There are several different kinds of glue that can be used. A very good choice of glue for most regular bowls is Weldwood Plastic Resin Glue. It is available in most hardware stores, building centers, or by mail-order catalogue suppliers. It is easy to mix, and is highly water resistant. It is not advisable to use an aliphatic resin glue. This type of glue seems to be more affected by ordinary humidity changes, and the rings tend to creep as the bowl gets older.

When using the plastic resin glue, be sure to coat both mating surfaces of the rings and base with glue. Also, be sure to assemble the bowl with the register lines and the word *top* aligned. Pressure is best applied

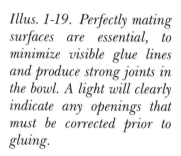

Illus. 1-19. Perfectly mating surfaces are essential, to minimize visible glue lines and produce strong joints in the bowl. A light will clearly indicate any openings that must be corrected prior to gluing.

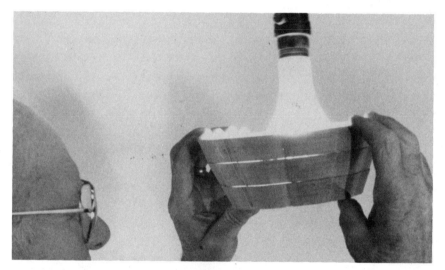

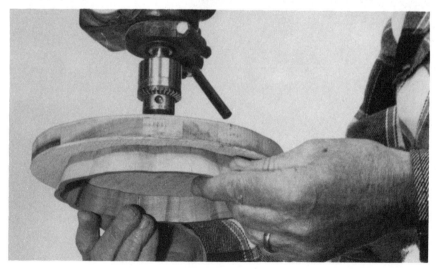

Illus. 1-20. Preparing the gluing surfaces of the rings using a special sanding disc in a drill press.

with a simple, shop-made clamping jig, as shown in Illus. 1-21. (See Chapter VII to make the jig.) However, you can also use other clamping methods.

It is also wise to check the bowl immediately after it is clamped, to be sure that the register lines are all lined up and the rings have not shifted. If necessary, release the pressure and reposition the rings.

When the bowl is removed from the clamp, you are ready to shape and finish it. Use shop-made sanding balls to work the inside surfaces, and flat sanding discs on the outside, convex surfaces. The procedures involved in making sanding balls are explained in Chapter VIII.

It is important that the flutes be of the same shape and size. If necessary, and to help achieve this objective, retransfer the lines back to the edge of the top ring from the inside or outside surfaces of the assembled bowl.

Illus. 1-22 and 1-23 show a glued-up bowl

with its subsequent rough-sanding completed. The success of the inside sanding operations depends entirely upon the use of the sanding balls designed especially for this work. Illus. 1-24 and 1-25 show the final shaping and smoothing work using the sanding balls.

Start sanding the inside using a 36-grit-abrasive-covered ball to rough-out the inside shape. Working from the bottom of the bowl upward, carefully define and shape each flute. Work one flute at a time, maintaining its specified width according to the rib markings transferred back onto the top ring. As you move from one flute to the next, you will soon develop a "feel" for shaping them, and will find that they can be shaped rather quickly.

After all the flutes are shaped, you are ready to use a 120-grit abrasive-covered ball. This ball is used primarily to smooth and remove the scratches left by the 36-grit sanding ball.

Illus. 1-21. The glue-coated rings are stacked and clamped in this shop-made bowl clamp. Note the use of a piece of wax paper or plastic film under the assembly; this ensures that the bowl will not inadvertently be glued to the clamp.

Illus. 1-22. The glued-up bowl, left, and the final abrasive shaping completed at the right.

21

Illus. 1-23. Bowl bottom details. "Foot" routing has been done to the bowl on the left. "Foot" routing is done before the rings from the blank are sawn. At right: A typical finished bowl bottom.

Illus. 1-24. Coarse, 36-grit abrasive on this special shop-made sanding ball gives the final shape to the insides of the bowl. Each flute will be shaped and defined.

Illus. 1-25. Once the final inside shape of the bowl has been established, use sanding balls with successively finer grits from 120 to 320 to do the final smoothing.

Next, use a 240-grit sanding ball to remove scratches left by the 120-grit ball and to straighten any slight deflections of the ribs between the flutes.

After you have sanded with the 240-grit ball, the bowl will look smooth inside. Use the 240-grit ball to slightly round off the ribs between the flutes; this gives the inside of the bowl a smoother shape and feel.

Next, work the outside of the bowl with a 5-inch-diameter flat disc sander. Shape the surfaces to match the curvature of the inside of the bowl (Illus. 1-26 and 1-27).

Use a simple shop-made calliper to maintain an even wall thickness (Illus. 1-29). Illus. 1-28 is a full-size pattern for the calliper. The two pieces can be made of aluminum, brass, or plastic approximately ³⁄₃₂ inch thick. Drill a hole in each one for a rivet or small bolt, and put them together.

After the calliper is assembled, adjust the points so that they line up with each other, and then file off the ends so that the points at both ends are close together when the calliper is closed.

This calliper is a positive-reading gauge. To use it, put either end on the bowl (Illus. 1-28). The wall thickness of one set of

Illus. 1-26. A 5-inch-diameter sanding disc with 36-grit abrasive is used to shape the outside of the bowl. It is recommended that you use a drill press with a speed not exceeding 1200 rpm.

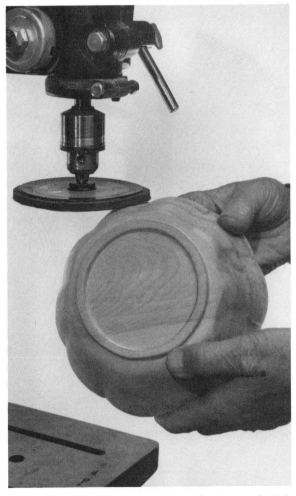

Illus. 1-27. Successively finer abrasives of 120, 240, and 320 grits are used to accentuate the flutes and smooth the outside of the bowl.

23

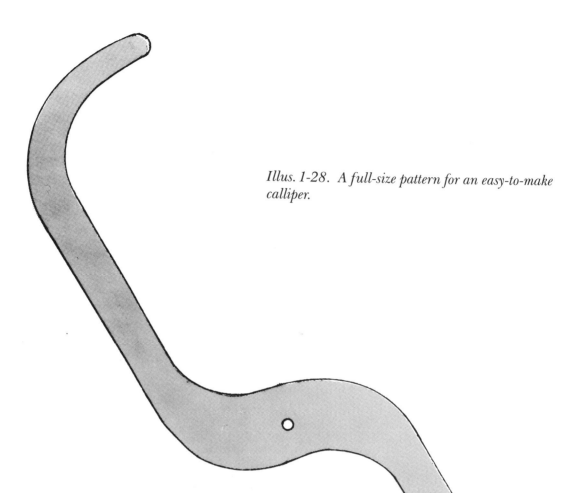

Illus. 1-28. A full-size pattern for an easy-to-make calliper.

Illus. 1-29. You can accurately check the wall thickness of the bowl at any point with this shop-made calliper.

points equals the gap remaining at the other end.

Shape the outside of the bowl, starting at the routed ridge or "foot" around the bottom of the bowl with 36-grit abrasive on the 5-inch-diameter flat-sanding disc (Illus. 1-26). Work all around the bottom of the bowl. This will be the thickest area of the bowl sides, and should be no thicker than $^{3}/_{16}$ inch, but not less than $^{1}/_{8}$ inch.

With the bottom foot roughed-out, sand each flute to about the $^{1}/_{8}$ inch thickness. As you progress from one flute to another, you will develop a "feel" for sanding each flute to $^{1}/_{8}$ inch. Progress to finer-grit abrasives as necessary to complete the shaping and smoothing operations.

Before beginning the final-sanding with 320-grit abrasive, cut or shape the scallops on the top edge. Extend all rib marks from the top edge downward onto the inside about $^{3}/_{16}$ inch on each rib with a pencil. Form the scallops with a coarse-grit sanding disc, or saw them on a scroll saw, as shown in Illus. 1-30.

Smooth the top edge using a 240-grit abrasive on the sanding ball or a flat sanding disc, as shown in Illus. 1-31. Round the

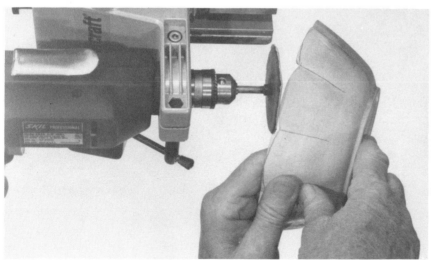

Illus. 1-30. Sawing the scallops shapes the top edge of the bowl.

Illus. 1-31. Shaping and smoothing the top-edge scallops with a sanding disc.

25

top edge slightly to eliminate sharp edges.

Now, complete the bowl by sanding all surfaces using 320-grit abrasives on a sanding ball and a flat sanding disc.

Give all surfaces a thorough visual inspection, to ensure that all minute scratches are removed. The project is ready for the final surface finish to be applied. Use whatever is your favorite finish or one that is strongly recommended. MINWAX Antique Oil gives a permanent finish. Apply five coats on very close-grained hard woods such as bloodwood, and seven coats on most United States hard woods. More information on finishes and finishing is given in Chapter XIV.

The preceding was an overview of the entire process of making a bowl. You should now have a good understanding of how to make any bowl shown in this book. You will learn how to proceed more quickly and simply with each new bowl you make. This craft becomes even more interesting when you start using inlays and employ some of the other bowl-decorating techniques described in later chapters.

Chapter II
Bowl Designs and Patterns

In this chapter, many types of bowls are described and illustrated. All are considerably different in their design or overall shape than the regular fluted bowl used as a demonstration example in the previous chapter.

A number of new designs (Illus. 2-1 and 2-2) with top-view patterns (Illus. 2-3) and corresponding sectional plans (Illus. 2-4) are provided full-size. Almost all of the bowl shapes shown in this chapter can be exactly duplicated from these details. Along with these specifications are other, optional

Illus. 2-1. A modified fluted bowl made from padauk wood. The modified flutes result in a wavy design without the typically sharp interior ribs of common fluted bowls like the practice bowl described in Chapter I. Note the undulating inlay—a technique described in Chapter XII.

Illus. 2-2. Another view of the same modified flute bowl, showing its wavy, scalloped top edge.

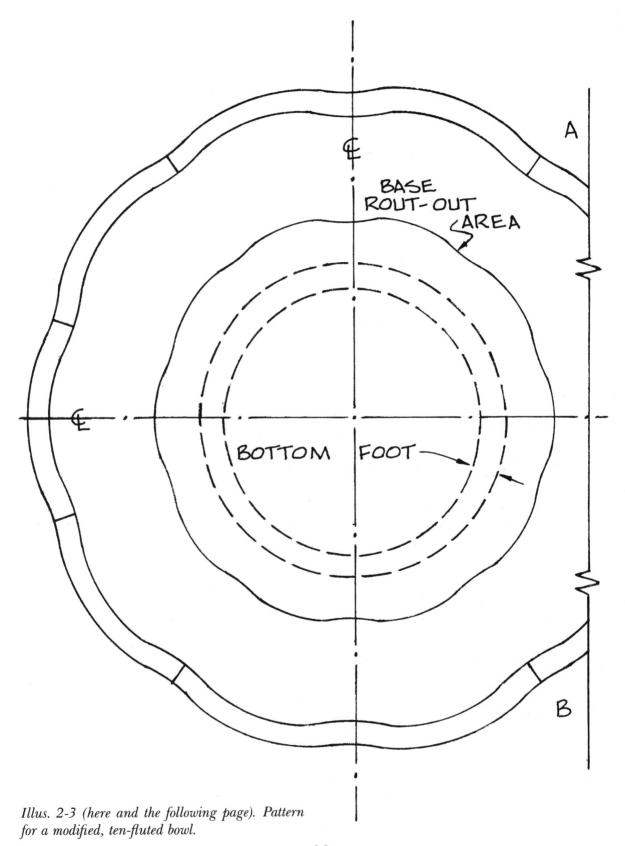

A

BASE
ROUT-OUT
AREA

BOTTOM   FOOT

B

*Illus. 2-3 (here and the following page). Pattern
for a modified, ten-fluted bowl.*

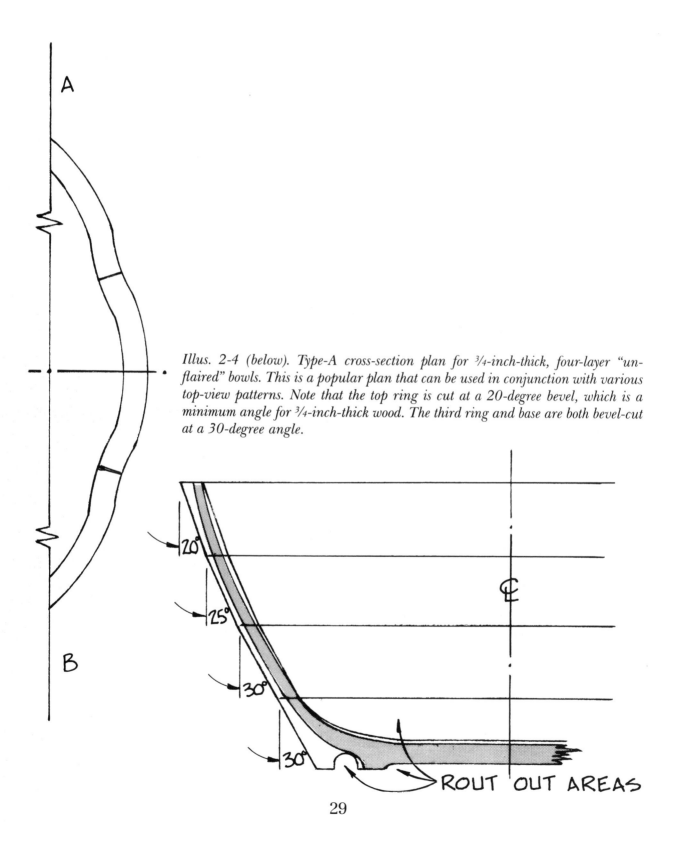

Illus. 2-4 (below). Type-A cross-section plan for ¾-inch-thick, four-layer "un-flaired" bowls. This is a popular plan that can be used in conjunction with various top-view patterns. Note that the top ring is cut at a 20-degree bevel, which is a minimum angle for ¾-inch-thick wood. The third ring and base are both bevel-cut at a 30-degree angle.

29

cross-sectional plans that can also be used with a variety of top-view patterns. Consequently, by combining the various alternatives of top-view patterns and sectional plan choices, you can dramatically increase the design possibilities.

However, before changing bowl sizes or putting together your own design combinations, carefully study this chapter or actually make some of the bowls according to the sizes given on these full-size drawings. This will help you avoid any problems you may encounter until you have more experience. Later in this chapter some guidelines for designing your own bowls are provided.

The most popular cross-sectional plan is the type-A plan as shown in Illus. 2-4. Note that this plan specifies using material ¾ inch thick, which is a size easily obtainable by the majority of woodworkers. The type-A cross section can be used with a variety of different top-view pattern designs, including the modified flute, ovals, rectangular-ovals, and lobe designs that are introduced in this chapter.

The type-A cross-section is "unflaired." This means that the wall of the bowl does not turn outward near the top edge of the bowl. Bowls with edges that do turn outward are referred to as "flaired." They can be slightly, moderately, or fully flaired.

It is important to remember that the lines on the top-view patterns indicating the base rout-out areas and the location of the bottom foot will change if you change the thicknesses of the rings. If, for example, you use a thicker material, the base rout-out diameter will increase. Therefore, it is necessary to use the correct cross-sectional plan (which will be specified) if you intend to produce the bowl shapes exactly as shown in the accompanying photographs using the top-view plans precisely as drawn.

MODIFIED FLUTED BOWLS

Bowls in this category have a "wavy" look to them. They are essentially developed from regular fluted designs, but the perimeter edges of their top-view patterns are slightly altered. The "dips" or "ribs" between the flutes are softened, so there are no sharp inside ridges as normally found on the insides of regular fluted bowls. Illus. 2-1 and 2-2 show a padauk bowl with a modified ten-flute design. Note that its top-edge scallop also has a wavy design. This bowl was made using the top-view pattern (Illus. 2-3) and the type-A cross-section plan (Illus. 2-4).

Illus. 2-5 gives the top-view plan for making a modified seven-flute bowl. The same type-A, unflaired-wall cross-section is recommended for making this bowl. This bowl can also be made in the regular fluted style similar to the demonstration bowl described in Chapter I. Refer to pages 53 and 54 for information pertaining to designing a seven-flute bowl.

Illus. 2-6 and 2-7 show two views of a modified eight-fluted bowl. It is made of walnut, with optional maple and walnut trim and inlay work. This bowl has the type-A cross section. No top-view pattern is provided here, because it is not much different than the modified seven-fluted pattern given in Illus. 2-5.

COMBINATION LARGE-AND-SMALL FLUTED BOWLS

Another popular alternative to regular fluted bowls is a bowl with a combination of

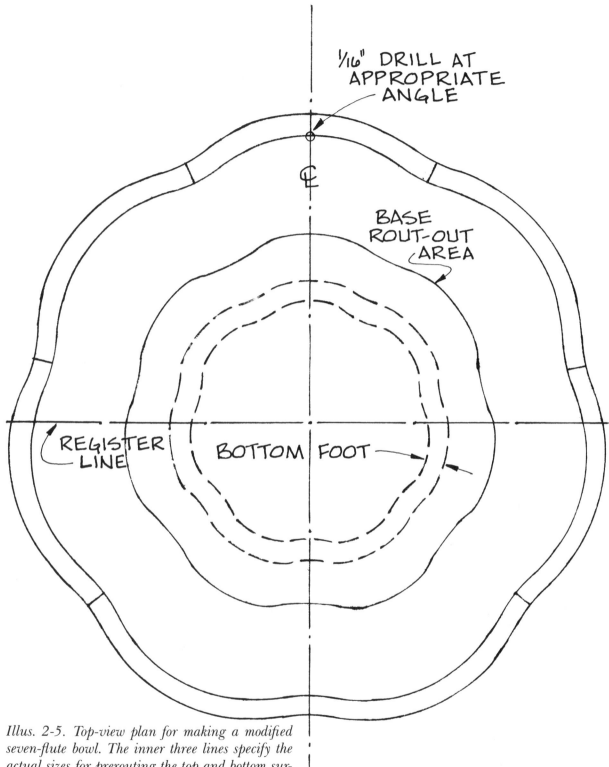

Illus. 2-5. Top-view plan for making a modified seven-flute bowl. The inner three lines specify the actual sizes for prerouting the top and bottom surfaces of the base blank. This bowl pattern is intended to also be used with the type-A cross section detailed in Illus. 2-4.

31

Illus. 2-6. A modified, eight-fluted walnut bowl with maple inlay and trim.

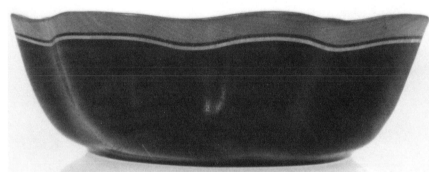

Illus. 2-7. This side view of the bowl in Illus. 2-6 shows how the maple and walnut veneer inlays undulate around the bowl. These special inlay techniques are also described in Chapter XII.

Illus. 2-8. This bowl, made from bloodwood, has large and small flutes. It is another one of many possible variations of fluted bowls. This bowl was made using the popular A-type cross section detailed in Illus. 2-4.

large and small flutes, as shown in Illus. 2-8. Illus. 2-9 gives the top-view pattern for this design. It consists of five 50-degree flutes with 1¾-inch-radius curvatures and five 22-degree flutes with 1½-inch-radius curva-tures. A suggested design for the top-edge scallop is also given in Illus. 2-9.

Illus. 2-10 and 2-11 show a purpleheart bowl with large and small flutes and op-tional inlay decoration. All bowls in this cat-

Above: The steps involved in creating bowls from scroll-sawn rings stack-laminated together. Just one flat board blank with a routed recess (far left) is sawn into bevelled rings to produce the bowl at the far right. Left, above: A fluted bubinga bowl with hollow base and deep-scalloped top edge. Left, below: A fluted bulbous bowl, made of walnut, with a plain top edge.

A

Above: A 12-inch fluted salad bowl, made of cherry, with a scalloped top edge. Left: A dry flower vase made of silky oak. Below: A patchwork bowl of cherry, walnut, and maple with a scalloped top edge.

Above: A rounded square bowl made of bloodwood and maple strips. Right: A dry flower vase made of bubinga. Below: A purpleheart fluted bowl with diagonal inlays of maple.

C

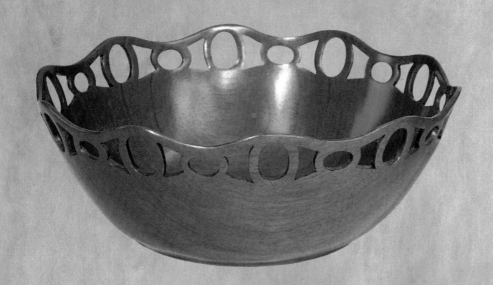

Above: A round bubinga bowl with fretwork trim. Center: A bulbous walnut bowl with fretwork trim. Below: This round bubinga bowl also has fretwork trim. Fretwork provides an ideal method for decorating wood bowls.

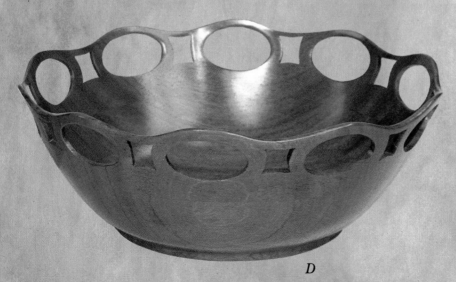

D

Above: A bloodwood bowl with small and large flutes and a scalloped top edge. Center: A round walnut bowl with diamond-shaped inlays of brass and bloodwood. Below: This black-walnut bowl has four large and four small flutes in combination with conical rings of maple and walnut veneer, to make the undulating inlays which parallel the scalloped top edge.

E

Above: A cherry bowl with round brass and bloodwood inlays. With the round inlays set in at an angle to the side of the bowl, they appear oval in shape. Left: This maple vase with bloodwood inlays and trim is essentially two bowls standing on edge, with a vertical layer of bloodwood between them. A bloodwood bottom is applied last. Below: A bulbous walnut bowl with a linking-chain inlay of maple.

Above: A flared-top, rectangular-oval bowl, made from bird's-eye maple, with a purpleheart inlay and a top-ring trim. Right: A round bulbous bowl made of black walnut. Below: A fluted, bulbous bowl, made of cherry, with a scalloped top edge.

G

Above: This group of bowls displays a variety of different shapes. Below: Three types of fluted bowls. The one on the left has the most basic design. It has equal-sized flutes and a scalloped top edge. The one in the middle has the same basic design, with added inlays and trim. The bowl on the right has large and small flutes. The blank is glued up so that each flute is made from a separate piece of wood. It also has a bloodwood inlay in its bottom.

H

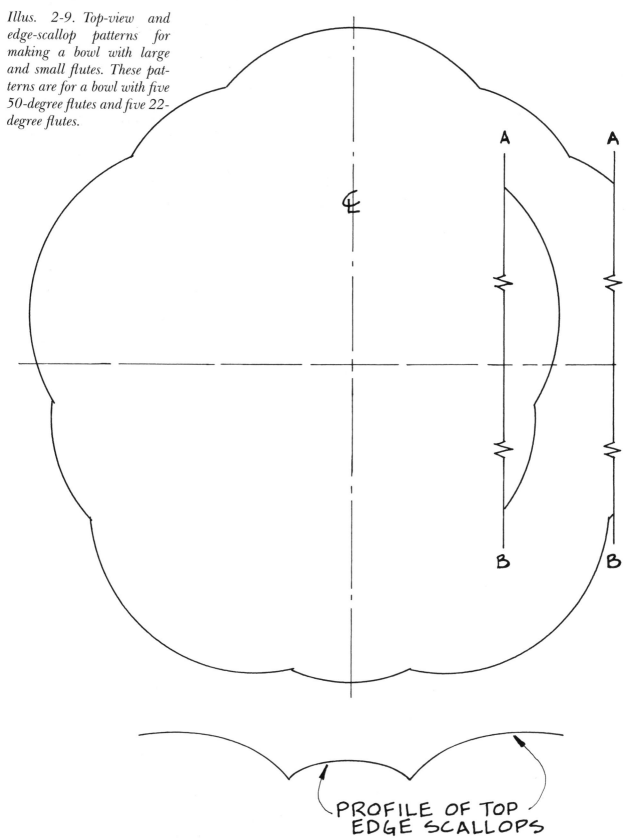

Illus. 2-9. Top-view and edge-scallop patterns for making a bowl with large and small flutes. These patterns are for a bowl with five 50-degree flutes and five 22-degree flutes.

A   A

℄

B   B

PROFILE OF TOP
EDGE SCALLOPS

33

Illus. 2-10. A large-and-small-fluted bowl made of purpleheart wood and with diagonal maple inlays.

Illus. 2-11. This view of the same bowl shows the inlay pattern and scalloped-edge designs. The bowl was cut diagonally three successive times after the rings were glued together. A layer of maple veneer was glued in to replace the wood lost due to the saw cuts. The bowl was then completed in the usual manner.

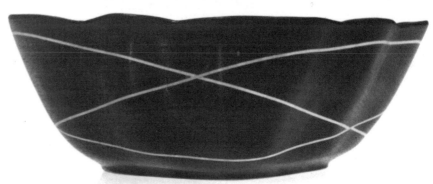

egory and described and illustrated here were made using the type-A cross-sectional plan (Illus. 2-4).

An entirely different approach to making a bowl with large and small flutes is shown in Illus. 2-12. The flat starting blank for making the rings begins as a glued assembly of wedged-shaped pieces of wood. Five 22-degree and five 50-degree wedge-shaped pieces are carefully fitted and glued together, as shown in Illus. 2-13. With this type of assembly, a hole would normally result in the bottom. To eliminate the bottom hole and to add some color, an inlay was set into the bowl blank before it was laid out or any of the rings sawn. The inlay became the bowl bottom, and the bowl was then com-

pleted employing the usual laminated-ring procedures.

It is interesting to note that this maple bowl has a unique grain pattern that was produced by selecting flat-sawed wood to make the initial wedge-shaped pieces. Bevel-sawing the rings created cut faces at right angles to the annual rings of the wood. This, in turn, produced a distinctive quarter-sawn grain pattern on all surfaces of the bowl.

Another walnut bowl with large and small flutes and spectacular, but optional, maple inlay work is shown in Illus. 2-14–2-16. This bowl was also made from ¾-inch-thick rings according to the type-A cross-sectional plan on page 29. The vari-

34

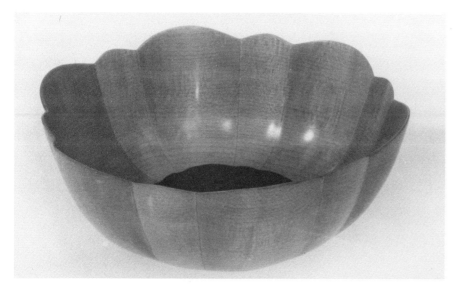

Illus. 2-12. This maple bowl with a bloodwood inlay on the bottom also has large and small flutes. First, flat-sawn triangular segments of maple were glued together to form the flat bowl blank. Then the center of the blank was inlaid with a piece of bloodwood before it was routed or sawn out. Once this flat bowl blank was prepared, the usual process of making ring-sawn laminations was employed.

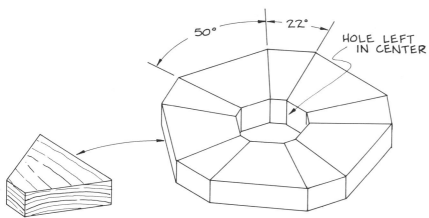

50° 22°

HOLE LEFT
IN CENTER

SEGMENTS CUT FROM
FLAT SAWN STOCK

Illus. 2-13. Here's how the bowl blank was prepared (before it was inlaid with bloodwood) to make the bowl shown in Illus. 2-12.

Illus. 2-14. This beautiful black walnut bowl has large and small flutes and features unusual inlay work.

Illus. 2-15. A top view of the same bowl. Note that the shape of the inlay in the bottom corresponds to the circumference shape of the bowl.

Illus. 2-16. Another view showing the side-view profile. Note the shallow scallop and the unusual inlaid ring of varying width. Chapter XII describes this special inlaying technique.

able width of the maple inlay around the bowl is intriguing to everyone who views this piece. The secret to this inlaying technique is revealed in Chapter XII, "Undulating Inserts."

BOWLS WITH MODIFIED LARGE AND SMALL FLUTES

Modifying the shapes of large and small flutes is still another design possibility. Illus. 2-17 and 2-18 show two views of a bubinga bowl. This bowl is intended to be shallow in depth. It consists only of three layers of ¾-inch-thick wood as specified by the type-D cross section shown in Illus. 2-21.

LOBED BOWLS

Bowls in this category have irregular, curved top-view profiles with no defined ribs, but still appear to have a planed division of a rounded form. Lobed bowls lend themselves well to a wide variety of cross-sectional shapes from unflaired to full flair. See Illus. 2-19–2-26 for plans incorporating designs with ¾-inch- and 1-inch-thick wood.

Illus. 2-17. This bowl, made of bubinga, has modified or softened large and small flutes, which create a distinctive look.

Illus. 2-18. This side view of the bubinga bowl in Illus. 2-17 shows a top-edge scallop design featuring "flats" along the upper edge. This bowl was made from a type-D cross section. (See Illus. 2-21.)

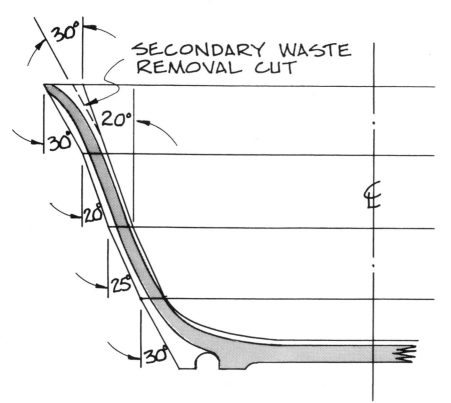

SECONDARY WASTE
REMOVAL CUT

30°

30°

20°

30°

20°

25°

30°

Illus. 2-19. This type-B cross-section plan can be used with ¾-inch-thick wood to make a four-layer bowl with a "medium" flair. Note that the top ring is actually bevel-sawn a second time on its inside to remove excess material, thereby roughing-out the flaired top edge of the bowl.

37

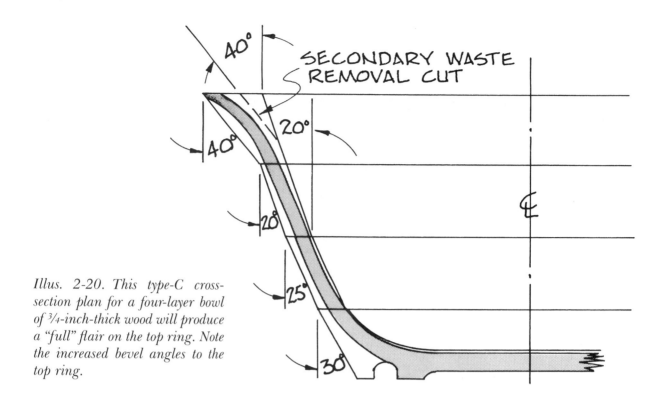

Illus. 2-20. This type-C cross-section plan for a four-layer bowl of ¾-inch-thick wood will produce a "full" flair on the top ring. Note the increased bevel angles to the top ring.

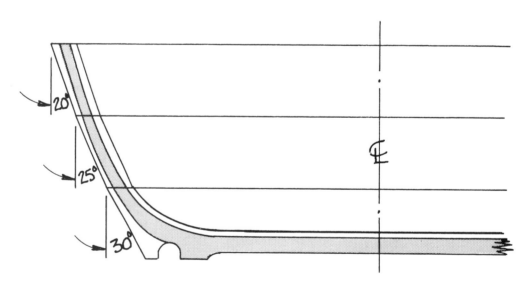

Illus. 2-21. This type-D cross-section plan for a three-layer bowl of ¾-inch-thick wood will produce a shallow, "unflaired" bowl.

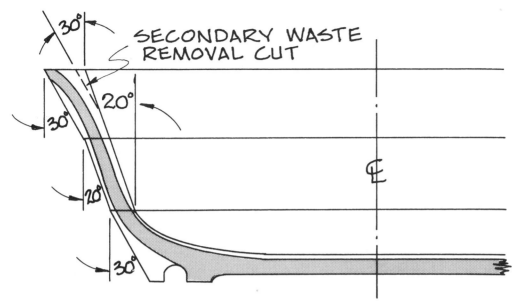

Illus. 2-22. This type-E cross-section plan for a three-layer bowl of ³/₄-inch-thick wood will create a "medium" flair on a shallow bowl.

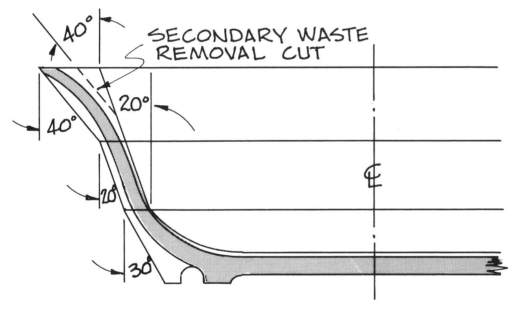

Illus. 2-23. This type-F cross-section plan for a three-layer bowl of ³/₄-inch-thick wood will produce a shallow bowl with a "full" flair.

39

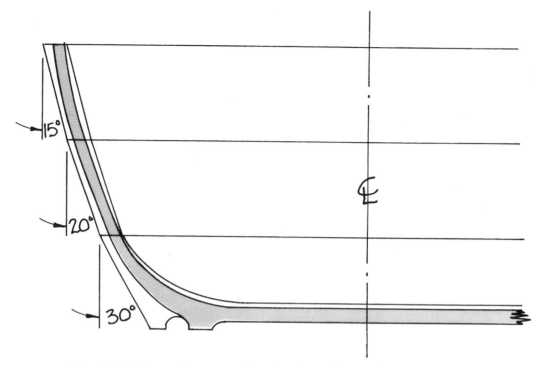

Illus. 2-24. A type-G cross-section plan for making a three-layer "unflaired" bowl of 1-inch-thick wood.

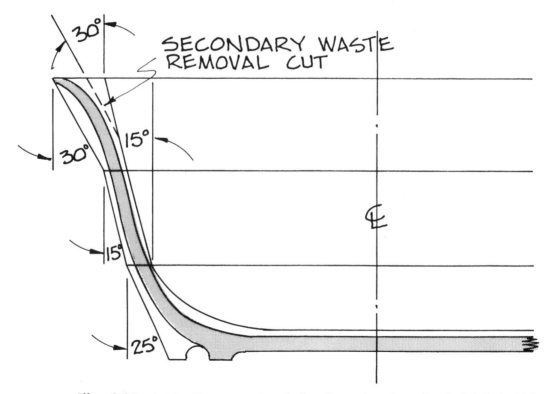

Illus. 2-25. A type-H cross-sectional plan for a three-layer bowl of 1-inch-thick wood and a "medium" flair.

40

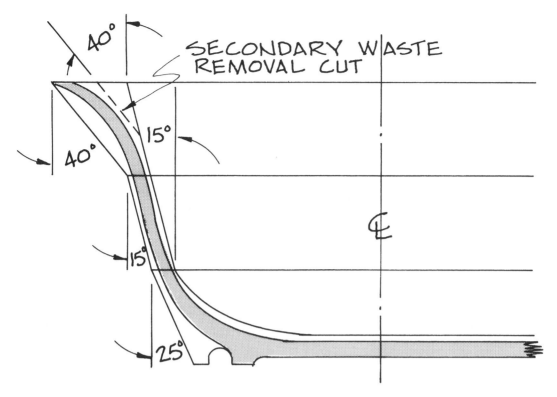

Illus. 2-26. A type-I cross-section plan for a three-layer bowl of 1-inch-thick wood with a "full" flair.

Illus. 2-27 shows a beautiful walnut lobed bowl with a dramatic inlay of 180 pieces of different types of wood. The popular A-type cross-section plan (page 29) was used to make this bowl, and the top edge was left unscalloped. Illus. 2-28 presents the top-view pattern used to make this bowl.

Illus. 2-27. This lobed walnut bowl has an inlay of 180 pieces of different kinds of wood sandwiched between maple veneer. It was made with a type-A cross-section plan, and its top edge was left unscalloped.

41

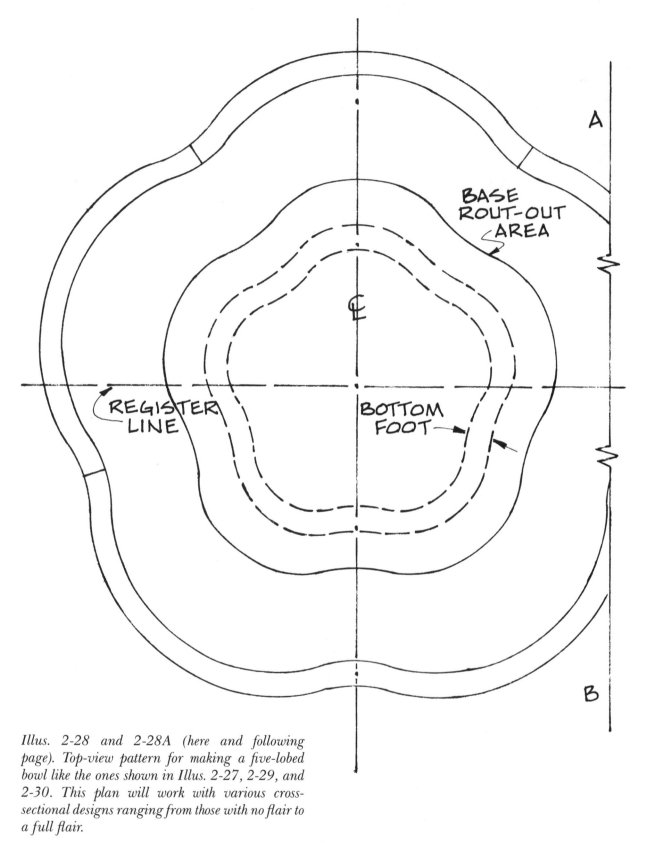

A

BASE
ROUT-OUT
AREA

℄

REGISTER
LINE

BOTTOM
FOOT

B

Illus. 2-28 and 2-28A (here and following page). Top-view pattern for making a five-lobed bowl like the ones shown in Illus. 2-27, 2-29, and 2-30. This plan will work with various cross-sectional designs ranging from those with no flair to a full flair.

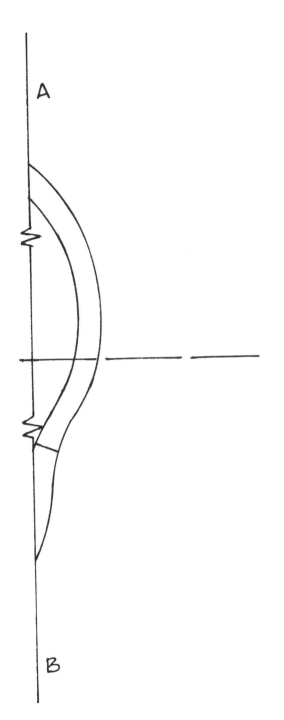

sectional plans. It has a total of four layers of 1-inch-thick rings, rather than three layers.

OVAL BOWLS

Oval bowls (Illus. 2-31 and 2-32) are very simple but extremely elegant bowls. They look best with flaired cross sections. The cherry bowl shown in Illus. 2-31 was made with the type-I cross-sectional plan (Illus. 2-26) and the top-view pattern in Illus. 2-33. To make a bowl exactly like this cherry bowl, start with a blank 1 inch thick.

Illus. 2-34 and 2-35 show a beautiful oval bowl of rosewood that incorporates a type-E cross section (Illus. 2-22). This type of cross section is used to make a fairly shallow bowl with a "medium" flair of three layers of ¾-inch-thick wood.

Oval bowls require very careful inside sanding, to ensure that continuous smooth and flowing curves will result. Dips and even shallow irregularities will be noticeable.

Illus. 2-29. A flaired, lobed bowl made of black walnut.

Another lobed bowl is shown in Illus. 2-29 and 2-30. This particular bowl was made by combining types A and I cross-

43

Illus. 2-30. Another view of the walnut lobed bowl that shows the dramatic effect of the wide, flairing top edge.

Illus. 2-31.This flaired bowl, made of cherry, has an oval-shaped top.

Illus. 2-32. This side view of a cherry oval bowl clearly shows the "full" flair of the top ring. A type-I cross-section plan was used to make this bowl.

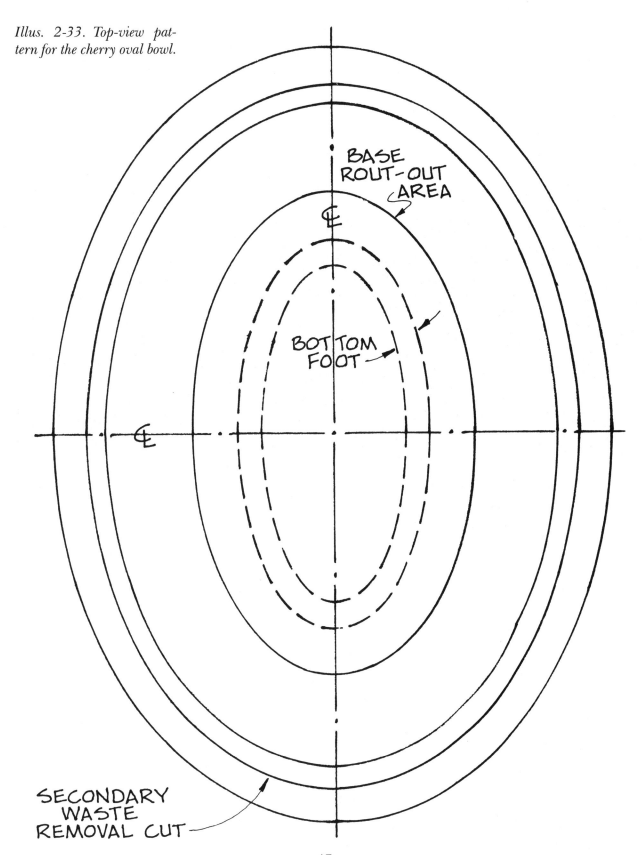

Illus. 2-33. Top-view pattern for the cherry oval bowl.

BASE
ROUT-OUT
AREA

℄

℄

BOTTOM
FOOT

SECONDARY
WASTE
REMOVAL CUT

45

Illus. 2-34. This rosewood oval bowl, made with the type E cross-section plan, has a "medium" flair. It was made from three-layer, ¾-inch-thick wood.

Illus. 2-35. This side view of the rosewood oval bowl shows the medium flair created by using the type E cross section.

RECTANGULAR-OVAL BOWLS

Rectangular-oval bowls are so named because their tops are rectangular-oval in shape (Illus. 2-36). The top-view plan (Illus. 2-37) for making this particular type of bowl is best used with the type-C cross section shown in Illus. 2-20. This gives the bowl a dramatic full flair around its top edge.

The rectangular-oval design is very suitable for adding optional inlays and trim work around the top edge of the bowl (Illus.

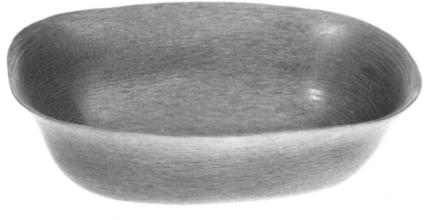

Illus. 2-36. A rectangular-oval bowl made of ¾-inch-thick fishtail oak. This bowl, created with the type-C cross-sectional plan, has a full flair.

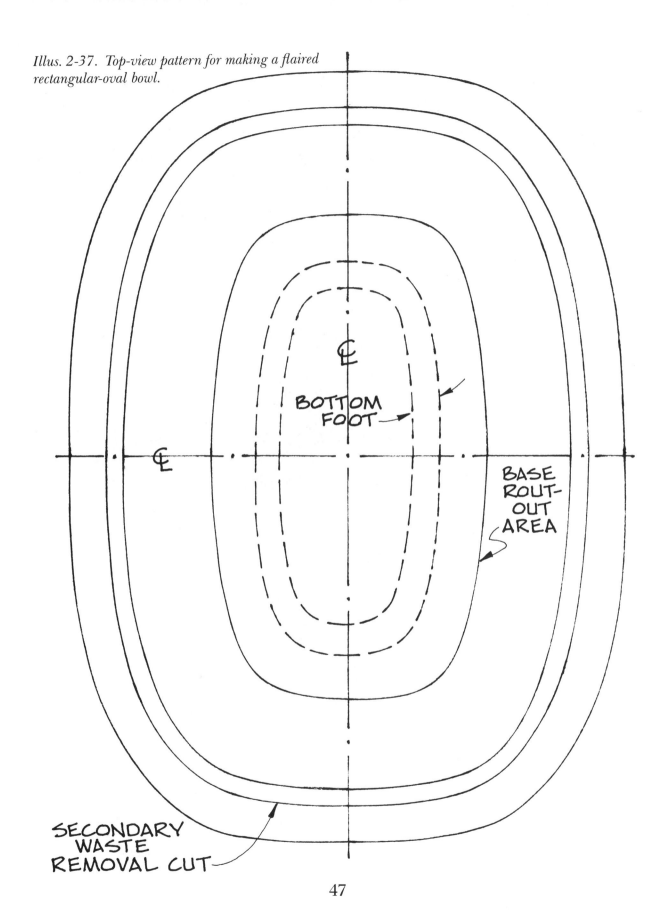

Illus. 2-37. Top-view pattern for making a flaired rectangular-oval bowl.

C⌀

C⌀

BOTTOM FOOT

BASE ROUT-OUT AREA

SECONDARY WASTE REMOVAL CUT

47

*Illus. 2-38. Another rectan-
gular-oval bowl. This one,
made of bird's eye maple, has
a purpleheart bottom inlay
and trim on its top, full-
flaired edge.*

*Illus. 2-39. This top view
clearly depicts the interesting
rectangular-oval shape.*

*Illus. 2-40. A bottom view.
Note the raised foot that is all
around the bowl, and the au-
tographed and dated signa-
ture by the bowl-maker.*

48

Illus. 2-41. A rectangular-oval bowl made of Australian fishtail oak, and with maple trim.

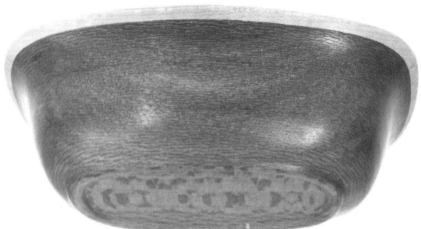

Illus. 2-42. A bottom view. Note the large wood rays visible in the oak. The top-edge maple inlay is made by reversing normal procedures. The oak bowl blank itself actually started as an inlay set into the surrounding maple trim ring.

2-38–2-40). Another, similar rectangular bowl with top-edge trim work is shown in Illus. 2-41 and 2-42. Refer to Chapter X, "Basic Inlays," which provides instructions on making bowls identical to these, if you wish.

BULBOUS BOWLS

Bulbous bowls (Illus. 2-43) look more like lathe-turned bowls than any of the other bowls described in this book. The term "bulbous" refers to the "bulb"-like shape of these bowls. The bulbous bowl can be round in shape, as shown in Illus. 2-43, or you can design it to be fluted.

If you have a wood lathe, you may elect to use it to finish-shape and sand the round

Illus. 2-43. A "bulbous" (bulb-shaped) bowl is another interesting bowl that can be made by stacked-ring lamination. This type of bowl, although round, can also be made to be of other shapes.

surfaces of bulbous bowls. They can be mounted to faceplates with double-faced tape. Otherwise, you can make round bulbous bowls without a lathe. Use the ball sanders on the inside surfaces and disc sanders on the outside surfaces, just as is normally done when making other, irregularly shaped bowls.

Bulbous bowls are made using type-J and K cross sections (Illus. 2-44 and 2-45). Think of making bulbous bowls as really making two bowls, one inverted over the other. One bowl is above the horizontal dividing line, and the other is below.

Some interesting grain patterns can be achieved if you begin with wood that is somewhat more than twice the thickness needed. Resaw it into two bowl blanks. Use one piece to make the top part of the bowl, and the other piece to make the bottom rings and base piece. Mark registration lines on all pieces so that they can be glued back together as they were in the original piece. The resulting bowl will appear as if it were made from one very large piece of wood.

When making fluted bulbous bowls, it is advisable to rout out the base so that it conforms to the top-view shape of the bowl. This step minimizes much of the extra sanding in the bottom of the bowl, which is more difficult to do with the partially closed top.

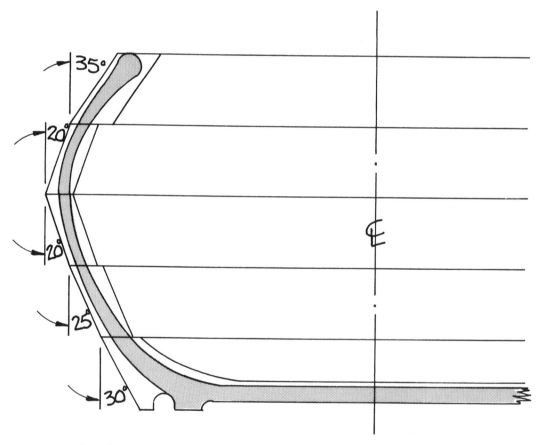

Illus. 2-44. A type-J cross-section plan for a five-layer bulbous bowl made of ³⁄₄-inch-thick wood. Bulbous bowls are best made by starting with wood slightly more than twice as thick as needed. Then resaw it, so you have one piece to make the rings for the top and another piece to make the bottom rings.

50

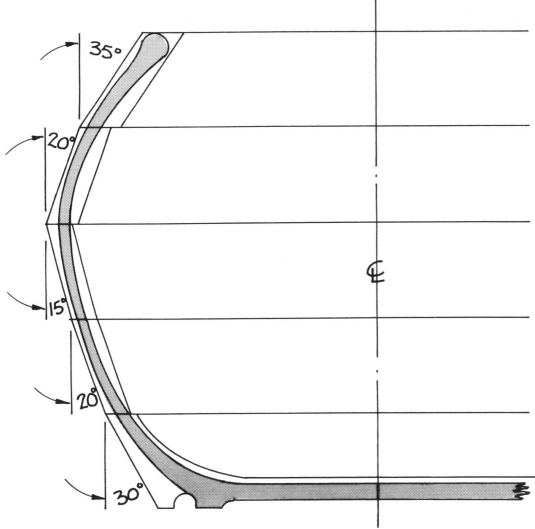

Illus. 2-45. A type-K cross-section plan for a five-layer bulbous bowl made from 1-inch-thick wood.

MISCELLANEOUS BOWL DESIGNS

Illus. 2-46–2-49 depict just a few of an endless variety of unusual shapes that the creative woodworker can use to make bowls. Virtually any conceivable shape that you can bevel-cut with a scroll saw can be incorporated into a bowl design. Soon you will be designing bowls of all shapes, sizes, and for various special uses.

DESIGNING BOWLS

If you want to design your own bowls, you can use all of the examples shown previously for guidelines. Designing your own bowls certainly adds to the pleasure and satisfaction of bowl-making. The bowls can be made as simple or as complex as you wish. Having some talents as a draftsman and some of the basic tools needed to develop plans and drawings will be helpful.

Making larger or smaller versions of the bowl plans in this book involves some design considerations that can be best accomplished with an office copy machine. The top-view patterns can be increased or decreased to any desired size. The cross-section drawings in this book can likewise be changed to adapt them to the particular thickness of wood you intend to use to make the bowl.

Most better copiers enlarge by 1 percent increments. For example, if the drawing in the book is 6 inches and you want to make a 7½-inch bowl, the plan would be enlarged 25 percent. If you want to make a 9-inch bowl, the plan would be enlarged 50 percent. Copiers enlarge up to a maximum of 200 or 300 percent, but are usually limited to 11-inch × 17-inch paper.

First and of foremost importance in developing your own designs are the horizontal and vertical registration lines that are basic to the plan. The intersection of these two lines is the center of the bowl. These register lines and the word *top* are used for ring alignment to maintain a consistent and natural grain pattern in the bowls.

Illus. 2-47. Here is another uncommonly shaped bowl. This dry-flower vase is made of maple, with bloodwood inlaid hearts on each side.

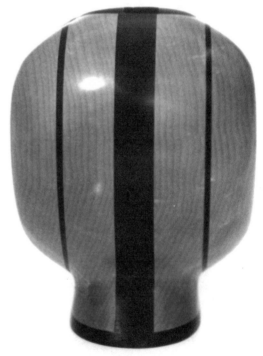

Illus. 2-46. This heart-shaped cherry-wood bowl is a good example of the wide range of various shapes that are possible with this kind of bowl-making technique.

Illus. 2-48. This end view more clearly shows how this bowl was made. Imagine two bowls standing vertically on edge, with a piece of ¾-inch-thick bloodwood glued between them. A thin layer of bloodwood is also glued between the maple rings and across the bottom.

52

Illus. 2-49. This oval-shaped offering tray was designed for a church.

An obviously important step is drawing the top-view, perimeter shape of the bowl. For example, if you are making a ten-flute bowl, you will have to divide a circle into ten sections. To draw radiused curvatures on the flutes, you need to develop appropriate centerlines that radiate from the center of the bowl. Generally, odd-numbered divisions are considered more artistic or pleasing to the eye than even ones. Dividing a circle into divisions of 9, 7, and 5 is logical.

However, dividing 360 degrees equally by seven is not usually very easily done. Illus. 2-50 shows a simple way to do it. First, draw an equilateral triangle with the radius of the circle as the length of the sides. The distance from the center of the circle to the middle of the opposite side is almost ⅐ of the circle. To compensate for the amount it is off, mark off the divisions of a circle with a divider inside the layout line, but just touching it, to divide it evenly.

When designing fluted bowls, it is necessary to consider the overall changing curvatures of the flutes as they progress from the top edge of the bowl towards the bottom. A flute's surface will have larger radiused curves at the top edge of the bowl than it does at the bottom of the bowl. This is because as the bowl gets smaller in size at the bottom, all of the corresponding flute curvatures are also reduced because of the ta-

pering of the sides towards the base or bottom of the bowl.

The shape and curvature of the flute also have to be satisfactory to the eye of the designer. And, just as importantly, remember that the flutes are best sanded with shop-made sanding balls that are 2½ inches in diameter. Smaller flute surfaces cannot be sanded with these devices.

Designing oval bowls is pretty much a straightforward effort of creating a visually pleasing top-view shape. Refer to drafting books for help, or simply change the outside size of the oval pattern in Illus. 2-33 to suit.

DESIGNING AND CHANGING CROSS SECTIONS

Designing and drawing your own cross-section plans also requires basic considerations. First, the depth of the bowl is, obviously, determined by the number of rings and the thickness of the wood used. Next, remember that the wood thickness affects the possible cutting angles of the rings. The cutting angles dictate the side-view shape of the bowl.

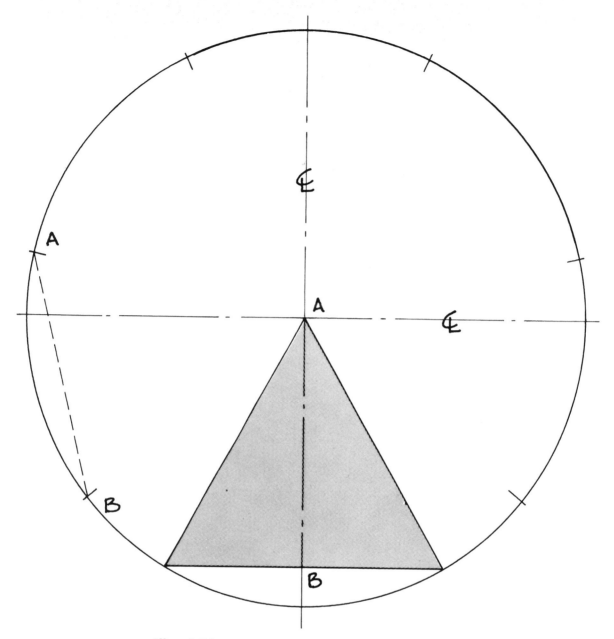

Illus. 2-50. How to divide a circle into seven equal parts. Draw an equilateral triangle with the radius of the circle as its sides, as shown. Distance A-B equals approximately a one-seventh division of the circle.

As a general rule, the minimum cutting angle for the first ring is 15 degrees for wood 1 inch thick or thicker, and 20 degrees for wood less than 1 inch thick. Wood ¾ inch thick is about the thinnest wood that can be satisfactorily used for making any bowl.

Normally, three rings and the base are cut when working with ¾-inch-thick wood, unless you are intentionally making a shallow bowl. Wood that is approximately 1 inch thick will usually have two rings and the base. If you have the wood, design the cross section according to the thickness of the wood being used. Otherwise, design the bowl cross section as you want it, and then find the wood to make it.

You can alter the cross-section plans for ¾-inch-thick wood slightly to compensate for different wood thicknesses by using an enlarging copy machine. Considering the 1 percent increment increase potential of most copiers, four 1 percent increments added to ¾ or .750 inch would be .30 or about ¹⁄₃₂ of an inch.

The source of your wood may also make a difference in its actual thickness. At the local lumber dealer, a 1-inch board is usually ¾ inch thick. A 1-inch or ⁴⁄₄ board with two surfaced sides obtained from a dealer specializing in hardwoods will usually be ²⁵⁄₃₂ inch thick. If your shop is equipped with a thickness planer, you can obviously mill wood to any thickness desired to match your own plan.

Another important factor to consider in bowl cross-section design relates to the size necessary to rout out the top and bottom recesses of the bottom piece. Woods of different thicknesses will dictate different base-size routing operations. The base-routing procedure is explored in detail in Chapter IV.

Finally, the top-edge design must be given some consideration. Sometimes the shape of the bowl is such that it is best left plain. Usually it is a good idea to shape scallops to correspond to the overall look of the bowl. A wavy bowl suggests and looks good with a wavy scallop. A perforated or fretted scallop is also a distinct possibility (Illus. 2-51).

Illus. 2-51. A bowl with a fretted top edge. See Chapter IX for full information about this unusual technique.

Chapter III
Wood Selection and Safety Techniques

Wood is our most useful and replaceable resource. With proper forest management, good wood should always be available. Some wood-harvesting practices, however, have recently been criticized, with much of the criticism directed to those of us who work with fine hardwoods. We have been accused of being responsible for destroying tropical rain forests because we use beautiful imported woods.

One big advantage to the method of making the bowls examined in this book is that it requires a minimum of wood. In fact, the techniques that are described should help to reduce the consumption of wood among fine-wood users. Conventional wood-turned bowls require massive solid blocks that are either of one piece or many pieces glued together. The laminated-ring techniques that we employ to "make" bowls yield a savings in both wood and cost of approximately 75 percent.

Use kiln-dried wood that ranges from 6 to 8 percent in moisture content. Avoid using locally air-dried woods without knowing their actual moisture content. Almost any properly dried wood can be used for making bowls. However, hardwoods are generally preferable over most softwoods. Hardwoods as a rule remain more dimen-sionally stable. Generally, they are also more attractive. Domestic and imported hardwoods come in a spectacular array of colors and distinctive figures (grain patterns). Natural wood colors range from pure white to stark black, with yellows, greens, browns, reds, purples, and other colors in between. Most specialty hardwood lumber dealers still have various kinds and colors of wood available.

Fine hardwoods can be obtained in most larger municipalities or by mail order for those who reside in rural areas. Check your Yellow Pages and the ads in major woodworking magazines. Most mail-order supply companies will sell small quantities to woodworkers. One such company, Owl Hardwood Lumber and Plywood Co., located in Lombard, Illinois, will fill orders as small as one board foot in quantity. Tables 3-1 and 3-2 list the company's typical inventory of domestic and imported species and stock thicknesses. Obviously, this listing changes with availability.

Note that fine hardwood lumber of a nominal one inch thickness (4/4) is reduced to $^{25}/_{32}$. Most lumberyards sell one-inch-thick softwoods dressed to a ¾ inch thickness. Board footage is calculated as Thickness × Width × Length, divided by 144.

Prices of wood constantly change, and always vary greatly from species to species. The price per board foot can range from around $1.50 (soft maple and willow) to over 25 dollars per foot for tulipwood, rosewood, and Gaboon and Macassar ebonies. One species of ebony (Ceylon) costs over $50 per square foot. Obviously, it is prudent to conserve every piece of wood.

An exceptionally good booklet describing the finest woods of the world is the *Fine Hardwoods Selectorama* (Illus. 3-1). This inexpensive publication has excellent color illustrations of major domestic and imported

DOMESTIC WOODS

Nominal Thickness Actual Thickness	3/4 1/2"	4/4 25/32"	5/4 1 1/16"	6/4 1 5/16"	8/4 1 3/4"	10/4 2 1/4"	12/4 2 3/4"	16/4 3 3/4"
Ash	x	x	x	x	x	x	x	x
Basswood	x	x	x	x	x	x	x	x
Beech	x	x						
Birch	x	x	x	x	x			
10" and wider	x	x	x	x	x			
Butternut	x	x						
Cedar	x	x						
Cherry	x	x	x	x	x	x	x	
10" and wider	x	x						
Cherry, figured	x	x						
Chestnut, wormy	x	x	x	x	x			
Coffee tree, Kentucky	x	x						
Cypress	x	x						
Elm, Red	x	x						
Gum, figured red	x	x						
Hickory/pecan	x	x	x	x	x			
Holly, blue-stained	x	x						
Holly, white	x	x						
Maple, hard	x	x	x	x	x	x	x	x
Maple, bird's-eye (high)	x	x	x	x	x			
Maple, bird's-eye (medium)	x	x	x	x	x			
Maple, figured	x	x	x	x	x			
Maple, soft	x	x	x	x	x	x		
Oak, red	x	x	x	x	x	x		
10" and wider	x	x	x	x	x	x		
Oak, red rift & quarter	x	x	x	x	x			
Oak, white	x	x	x	x	x			
10" and wider	x	x	x	x	x			
Oak, white rift & quarter	x	x	x	x	x			
Pecan (see hickory)								
Poplar	x	x	x	x	x	x	x	x
Walnut	x	x	x	x	x	x	x	
10" and wider	x	x	x	x	x	x	x	
Walnut, claro	x	x	x					
Willow	x	x						

All lumber is sold by the board foot (except thickness under 1/4, which is sold by the square foot).

Tables 3-1 and 3-2 (following page). A list of the wood species available by mail order from the Owl Hardwood Lumber and Plywood Company. The columns marked with an x indicate actual thicknesses available or thicknesses that can be made by reducing stock from the next greater thickness.

Nominal Thickness Actual Thickness	3/4 1/2"	4/4 25/32"	5/4 1 1/16"	6/4 1 5/16"	8/4 1 3/4"	10/4 2 1/4"	12/4 2 3/4"	16/4 3 3/4"
Afrormosia	x	x						
Amaranth								
(purpleheart)	x	x	x	x	x			
Autocarpus								
Hiroshita	x	x						
Balsa	x	x	x	x	x	x	x	x
Beefwood	x	x	x	x				
Benge	x	x	x	x				
Bubinga	x	x	x	x	x	x	x	x
Camphorwood	x	x						
Cocobolo	x	x	x	x	x			
Ebony, Ceylon	x	x	x	x	x			
Ebony, Gaboon	x	x						
Ebony, Macassar	x	x	x	x	x			
Guineah	x							
Imbuia	x	x						
Jatoba (Braz. Chy.)	x	x						
Jelutong	x	x	x	x	x	x	x	x
Koa	x	x						
Lacewood	x	x	x	x	x			
Laurel, East Indian	x	x	x					
Lignum Vitae	x	x	x	x	x	x		
Limba	x	x	x	x	x	x	x	x
Mahogany, African	x	x	x	x	x	x	x	
Mahogany, Honduras	x	x	x	x	x	x	x	x
Mahogany,								
Philippine	x	x	x	x	x			
Makore	x	x						
Makore, figured	x	x						
Mansonia	x	x						
Moradillo	x	x	x	x	x			
Padauk	x	x	x	x	x			
Parrotwood	x	x	x	x	x			
Pau D'Arco	x	x	x	x				
Primavera	x							
Primavera,								
figured	x							
Rosewood, Brazilian	x	x						
Rosewood,								
East Indian	x	x						
Rosewood, Honduras	x	x						
Rosewood, Santos	x	x						
Rosewood, Swartzia	x	x	x	x	x			
Satinwood, Nigerian	x	x	x	x	x			
Sepele	x	x						
Sharkwood	x	x						
Teak	x	x	x	x	x	x	x	
Tulipwood	x	x						
Walnut, African	x	x	x	x				
Walnut, Australian	x	x						
Wenge	x	x	x	x	x			
Yew, English	x	x						
Zebrawood	x	x	x	x	x			

Table 3-2.

Illus. 3-1. This booklet published by the Fine Hard-wood/Veneer Association provides excellent color photos and descriptions of most domestic and popular imported hardwoods.

woods. It gives the woods, their countries of origin, their scientific names, their physical properties, and their availability. This booklet also provides a price range classification. If you want a wood for a very special bowl, refer to this booklet. It is available from The Fine Hardwood/Veneer Association, 5603 West Raymond St., Suite O, Indianapolis, IN 46241. The price is $12.00.

For your first bowl, use a piece of domestic hardwood such as birch, cherry, soft maple, or walnut. Any suitable piece left over from a previous woodworking project will work.

Selecting a special piece of wood to take advantage of some of its special characteristics can add much to the resulting beauty of a bowl. For example, it is often advantageous to select a board for the bowl blank that is cut in such a way that the resulting grain pattern on the sides of the bowl will have a quarter-sawn figure. This will help immensely to camouflage the horizontal glue lines. In many cases, the glue lines are hardly detectable with the naked eye, giving the illusion of a hand-carved bowl that was made from one massive block of wood (Illus. 3-2 and 3-3).

Usually, a plain or flat-sawn bowl blank as shown in Illus. 3-4 will provide the most favorable results. When the rings are bevel-sawn, their cut surfaces are almost perpendicular to the growth rings; this gives the best effect. Quarter-sawn face grains on a bowl also emphasize the wood rays of

Illus. 3-2. The naturally fine grain figure of this bloodwood bowl, coupled with a "quarter-sawn" style of side-wall grain pattern, makes the glue lines almost totally invisible.

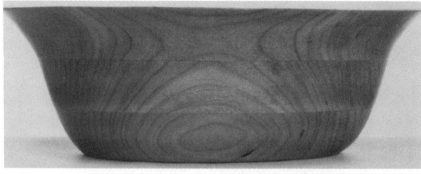

Illus. 3-3. A side view of this cherry bowl with a flat-sawn grain pattern on the side walls tends to show glue lines more. However, note how effectively the grain pattern flows from layer to layer.

Illus. 3-4. Rings cut out of this plain or flat-sawn board will have a quarter-sawn grain pattern on their surfaces.

Illus. 3-5. The quarter-sawn grain in the wood used on these vases hides the glue lines. The vase on the left is made of Australian silky oak. The vase on the right is made of African bubinga.

woods—some more so than others. Silky oak is a good example (Illus. 3-5).

Sometimes, due to the nature of wood itself, it's impossible to hide the glue lines. Beefwood, for example, darkens at its surface, which tends to emphasize the gluing area (Illus. 3-6).

One very unusual bowl with quarter-sawn graining all around it is shown in Illus. 3-7. The center of the bowl blank was routed through, and an inlay was prepared and glued in place (Illus. 3-8).

Some species have defects and growth traits that result in very interesting grain patterns. The following labels are used to describe woods with these special conditions: figured, butt cut, crotch, swirl, bird's-eye, curly, fiddleback, fiddleback mottle, peanut shell, beeswing and burl. Burl, bird's-eye, and curly (as in maple) are labels used to describe conditions supposedly caused by genetic defects in the species. Other conditions actually result from the way the board is sawn from the tree.

Some defects may appear after work on the bowl has begun. Small, dark lines and pitch pockets may reveal themselves once the board is cut into. Cherry and maple are two notable woods that will exhibit these defects at inopportune stages of the bowl's development.

Some species of wood can be used to make exceptional-looking bowls. Fishtail oak, lacewood from Australia, and purpleheart from Mexico, Central America, and Brazil are just a few interesting woods that make stunning bowls with very favorable figures (grain patterns).

Bloodwood and purpleheart are two colorful and beautiful woods. Both are very brittle and will shatter easily if dropped. Bloodwood, as its name implies, is bright-red. Purpleheart is an interesting wood that appears to be naturally brown, but turns purple upon being machined.

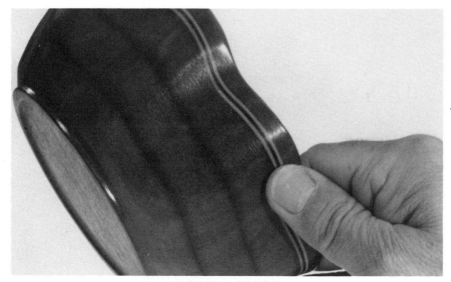

Illus. 3-6. The lamination glue lines are highlighted on this bowl of South American beefwood. This is because beefwood darkens on its surface after machining.

Illus. 3-7. This unusual bowl has quarter-sawn grain all around it, emphasizing the wood rays and the fine figure of maple.

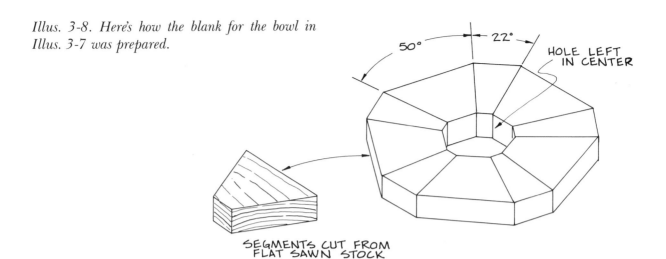

Illus. 3-8. Here's how the blank for the bowl in Illus. 3-7 was prepared.

50° 22° HOLE LEFT IN CENTER

SEGMENTS CUT FROM FLAT SAWN STOCK

SAFETY TECHNIQUES

Woodworkers should follow the same prudent safety precautions when making bowls that they follow for any woodworking activity. Never use any power tool when tired, distracted, or under the influence of medication. Always wear eye and hearing protective devices. Do not cut or machine small pieces of wood without safety fixtures and jigs as dictated by the job(s) at hand. Always respect all power tools, and refer to manuals and books for their proper care, adjustment, and operation.

A very serious problem, and one that's potentially very hazardous when working certain kinds of wood, is dust. Many woods can be very toxic, and reactions can vary from person to person. Irritations to the eyes, nose, sinus cavity, and the respiratory system can often be traced to dust and/or just the odor or scent of some woods.

The use of a good dust protector or respirator can prevent and eliminate most respiratory problems. One type highly recommended is manufactured by the 3-M Company (Illus. 3-9). This dust protector is not only very comfortable, it also does not steam up eyeglasses, an occurrence that can be dangerous when working around power equipment.

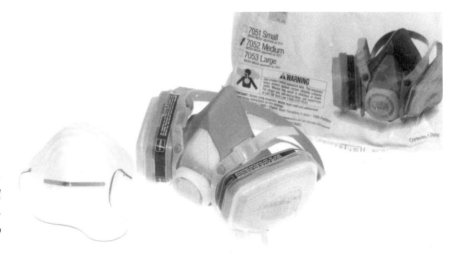

Illus. 3-9. A dust mask (left) or a respirator (right) should be worn as dictated by the operation at hand or the shop environment.

62

Chapter IV
Using a Router

The router provides three essential functions in the bowl-making process described in this book. First, it is used to begin the process by routing excess material from both the top and the bottom surfaces of the bowl blank (Illus. 4-1–4-3). These vital preliminary operations actually shape or form the inside and outside bottom surfaces of the bowl(s). Secondly, the router can be used to make very accurately cut templates used for performing these jobs quickly and precisely. Finally, the router is used to make many of the various kinds of bowl inlays and decorations described in detail in later chapters.

The information presented in this chapter is directed towards woodworkers who have some experience with routers and understand basic router operations. If not, refer to the books *Router Handbook* or *Router Basics*, both by Sterling Publishing Co.

TYPE OF ROUTER

Use either a plunge or fixed-base router with a ¼-inch-diameter collet or larger. The controlled and perfectly vertical bit-entry features of a plunge router offers some distinct advantages in template-routing and inlay work.

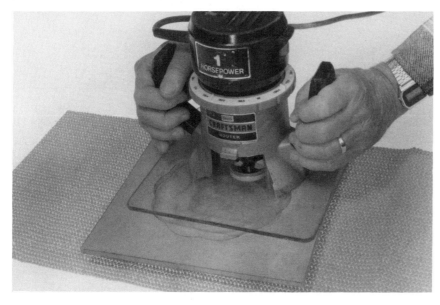

Illus. 4-1. The first operation is to rough-out the area that will become the inside bottom of the bowl. A template guides the router, which is mounted with a special shop-made router base and a template guide. The template is tacked to the bowl blank with two headless nails at opposite corners. Using one of the new, non-slip router pads eliminates the interference of clamps.

Illus. 4-2. Routing the upper surface of the bowl blank to remove excess material. This is the first operation performed on the bowl blank. The bit and router are actually guided by a template and a template guide on the router base.

Illus. 4-3. Make a second routing pass to achieve the final depth. Note: This cut is made with a size compensator that fits over the template guide; this reduces the size of the routing area.

SAFETY TECHNIQUES

Regardless of which type or brand of router you have, be certain to observe all of the recommended safety precautions. Always wear eye, ear, and respiratory protective devices. Be sure to use sharp bits so that you don't burnish the surfaces, making subsequent sanding more difficult. Regularly touch up the bits' cutting edges; this keeps them sharp longer. Refer to the book *Sharpening Basics*, published by Sterling Publishing Co., to learn how to do this.

ROUTER BASE PREPARATION

Even though you can perform all the operations described in this chapter with a light-duty router that has a ¼-inch-diameter collet capacity, the router should be fitted with a base that's larger than its regular factory base (Illus. 4-4 and 4-5).

Make a router base that is at least 9 inches square from ¼-inch-thick clear plastic. Polycarbonate plastic is more durable and easier to machine than acrylic or Plexiglas™.

Illus. 4-4. A view showing the shop-made plastic router base with the 1⅞-inch-outside diameter (O.D.) template guide, which is made from 1½-inch-PVC plastic pipe and cemented to a rabbeted lip in the base. Also shown is another plastic ring. This ring, which increases the outside diameter of the template guide, is referred to as a template-guide size compensator.

¼ × 9 × 9 POLYCARBONATE PLASTIC

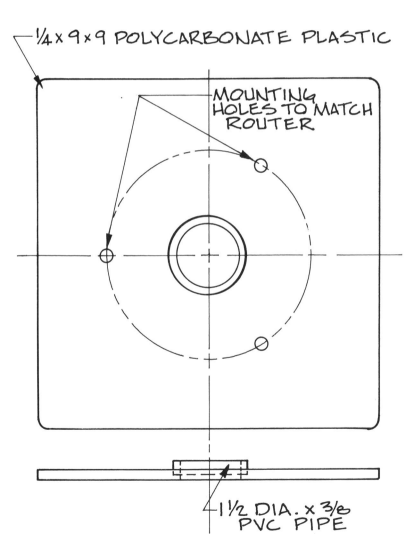

MOUNTING HOLES TO MATCH ROUTER

1½ DIA. × ⅜ PVC PIPE

Illus. 4-5. The details for making a router base with integral template guide to accommodate the large (1-inch radius) bit.

Template Guide

The router base must be adapted to carry a template guide that is larger than any currently on the market. This template will have to accommodate the large bits that will be used (Illus. 4-2 and 4-3). Center a piece of plastic pipe over the router collet and affix it with acrylic cement into a rabbeted lip machined into the new router base. Make the template guide from a ⅜-inch length of 1½-inch I.D. (inside diameter) PVC pipe which has a 1⅞-inch O.D. (outside diameter).

There are different ways to make the hole in the router base and rabbet it for the PVC template, but using a router is perhaps the easiest. If necessary, refer to the book *Router Jigs and Techniques*, Sterling Publishing Co., for more information about these procedures and those for making your own circle-routing jigs.

Template-Guide Size Compensators

Removable sleeves that fit over the template guide fitted into the router base, to increase its outer-diameter size, are named "size compensators." Installing or removing a size compensator automatically shifts the cutting location of the bit as it relates to the guiding edge of the template. With a size compensator placed over the template guide, the bit cuts farther from the template; when the size compensator is removed from the template guide, the bit follows closer to the template (Illus. 4-4 and 4-6–4-8).

Template-guide size compensators can be made to any diameter desired. (See Illus. 4-15 on page 71.) Size compensators are secured to the template guide with allen setscrews (6–32 × ¼ inch). A hole is drilled with a No. 36 bit and tapped horizontally

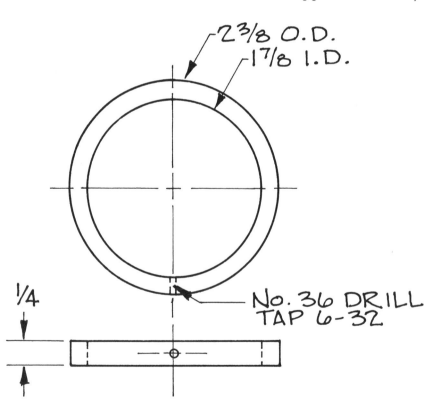

Illus. 4-6. Make this size-compensator sleeve from a PVC plastic bushing (a 1½ to 2-inch reducer). It will slip over the template guide of the router, increasing its outside diameter approximately ½ inch.

Illus. 4-7. This view shows how the size compensator functions. The size compensator is simply a removable ring which fits over the template guide so the bit will cut farther away from the edge of the template.

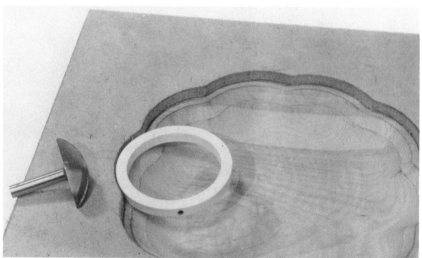

Illus. 4-8. The template-guide size compensator is used when routing approximately the last half of depth to complete the inside routed area on the bowl blank.

through one wall of the sleeve, as shown in Illus. 4-6.

The essential advantage of using a template-guide size compensator is that it allows you to make two different lines of cut that are perfectly parallel to each other using just one template or other types of guide. Size compensators function much like the inlay bushings described in Chapter XI, in that they increase the outside diameter of the template guide.

TEMPLATES

Just two templates are needed to rout the bowl blank. One is used for the top surface, and one for the bottom surface of the bowl blank. The templates must be made of the appropriate inside shape, and correctly sized. Simple bowls and bowls that are completely round require templates with true, round openings (Illus. 4-9). Bowls with more detailed oval, fluted, or lobed designs often require templates that conform to

67

Illus. 4-9. All routing templates should have registration lines (and a reference point marked "Top") that are aligned with the reference lines drawn on the bowl blank.

the top-view shape of the bowl (Illus. 4-10–4-12).

Templates are best made from ¼-inch-thick tempered hardboard or plywood that is approximately the size of the bowl blank or slightly larger, as required. Adjust and cut out the template's inside opening to allow for the offset of the bit, which is the distance the cutting circle of the bit is away from the template as the router template guide rides against it.

A simple formula to determine the overall inside opening size of the template is as follows: The desired routed-out area diameter plus the outside-diameter of the template guide minus the cutting diameter of the router bit equals the required inside-diameter opening for the template.

A simpler way to determine the inside diameter of the template when routing out the top surface of the bowl blank is to just add ⁵⁄₁₆ inch to the diameter (1⅞ inches for the template guide minus 1⁹⁄₁₆ inches for the router bit). To make a round template for routing the bottom of the bowl blank, simply add ³⁄₁₆ inch to the diameter of the routed section (⁷⁄₁₆ inch for the template guide minus ¼ inch for the router bit). *Note:* The diameter of the routed area on the bottom of the bowl blank will be ½ inch larger in diameter than the outside diameter of the foot on the bowl because you are also routing around the outside of the foot. You can cut out templates with the router using a circle jig, or with a scroll saw, if you are careful.

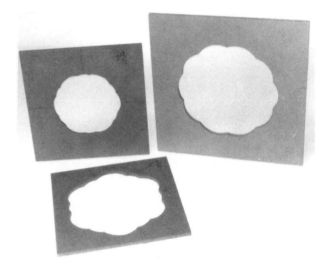

Illus. 4-10. Typical templates made from ¼-inch-thick tempered hardboard.

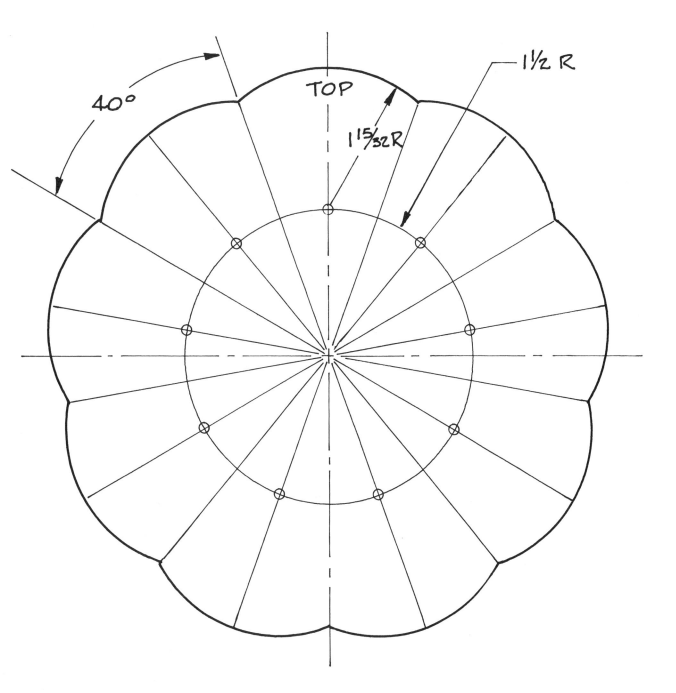

Illus. 4-11. A typical plan (pattern) for making an irregularly shaped template for routing the upper surface of the bowl blank. This plan is actually for a 9-flute bowl, shown on page 125.

Illus. 4-12. A circle-cutting jig on the router can be used to make templates with simple round openings. More complex templates, such as this one for a fluted bowl, can be made with circle jigs that will cut a relatively small radius as shown.

ROUTING PROCEDURES

The routed area cut into the upper surface of the bowl blank becomes the inside bottom of the fully assembled bowl. For this operation, use a 1-inch-radius cove bit, available from Sears (No. 9GT-25526), as shown

in Illus. 4-2 and 4-3, along with the appropriate template.

Since much material must be removed, remove it in two stages. First, cut away about half of the overall required depth in as many multiple passes as necessary or as dictated by the power of your router. Complete the routing to the final depth the same way, but use the size-compensator sleeve over the template guide. This will reduce the routed area only about ½ inch. However, this leaves a far more favorable wall contour for the ball-sanding operation that will be done later.

Routing the bottom of the bowl blank is an optional operation, but one highly recommended because it gives the bowl a very distinct and professional look, even though the bottom is seldom seen. All of the routing on the bottom of the bowl blank can be done entirely with a ¼-inch-diameter roundnose (corebox) bit.

The essential purpose of routing the bottom of the bowl blank is to create a raised lip around the bowl. This raised lip is referred to as the "foot" of the bowl. You can complete the foot-routing operation using your regular factory router base, suit-

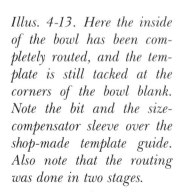

Illus. 4-13. Here the inside of the bowl has been completely routed, and the template is still tacked at the corners of the bowl blank. Note the bit and the size-compensator sleeve over the shop-made template guide. Also note that the routing was done in two stages.

70

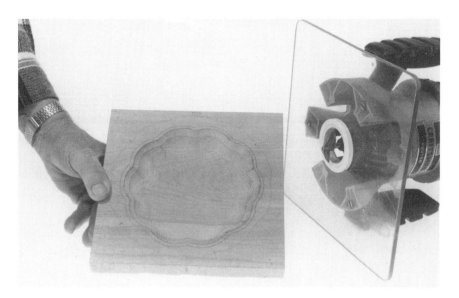

Illus. 4-14. The routing has been completed on the upper surface of the bowl blank.

ably fitted with any brand of a number of commercially available ⁷⁄₁₆-inch-outside-diameter template guides. You will also have to use a special shop-made template-guide size compensator and one shop-made hardboard template (Illus. 4-15 and 4-16).

Usually, the foot on less-complicated bowls will be round. The foot can also be made to "zig" in and out, to conform to the top-view shape of the bowl as desired. The routed area inside the foot is removed with a 1⁷⁄₁₆-inch-outside-diameter size compensator secured over the standard ⁷⁄₁₆-inch-outside-diameter template guide. Removing it from the template guide shifts the cut close to the guiding edge of the template, leaving a ¼-inch-wide uncut ridge or foot all around the bottom.

Illus. 4-15. Routing the bottom side of bowl blank requires these following devices: a template, a template guide, a template-guide size compensator (above), and ¼-inch corebox bit.

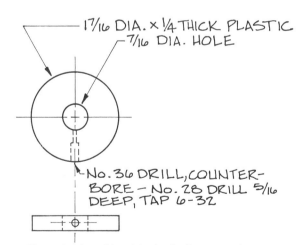

Illus. 4-16. This 1⁷⁄₁₆-inch-diameter size compensator is machined from ¼-inch-thick plastic to fit over a standard ⁷⁄₁₆-inch outer-diameter commercially available template guide. It is drilled (with a No. 36 drill) and tapped to receive a 6-32 allen setscrew.

71

Chapter V
Angle Blocks

Many drill presses do not have tilting tables. In such cases, angle blocks are helpful devices used to drill angular starting holes for scroll-sawing the insides of the bowl rings (Illus. 5-1). A set of four simple blocks (Illus. 5-2) permits you to drill starting holes at any of these angles: 10, 15, 20, 25, 30, 35, and 40 degrees.

A basic set of angle blocks consists of four tapered blocks. Make one with a 10-degree taper, one with a 15-degree taper, and two blocks with 20-degree tapers to complete the set (Illus. 5-3). Use any inexpensive softwood. Glue-up two layers of 1⅛-inch-thick shop pine or three layers of any available ¾-inch-thick wood to produce a total thickness of 2¼ inches. This becomes the workpiece supporting surface.

Depending upon the kind of bowl and the drilling angle(s) required, the angle blocks are used either singularly or in combinations (one on top of another), as shown in Illus. 5-4. This gives you the capability to drill in 5-degree increments between 10 and 40 degrees. The blocks are connected to each other with two dowel pins. To ensure that any one block can be fitted to any other block, drill all of the dowel pin holes at the very same spacings.

An easy-to-make drilling guide (template), as shown in Illus. 5-5, ensures that each set of holes will be drilled the same on each surface of each block. Drill all of the mating holes on the drill press. Use a drill-press vise or a hand-screw clamp to support the surface horizontally and at right angles to the bit.

Two other dowel pins placed side by side on the top surface of each block keep the workpiece from sliding during the actual ring-drilling operation (Illus. 5-1).

Illus. 5-1. An angle drilling block being used to drill a starting hole.

72

Illus. 5-2. This set of four softwood blocks will support work on the drill press for angle-drilling in 5-degree increments from 10 to 45 degrees.

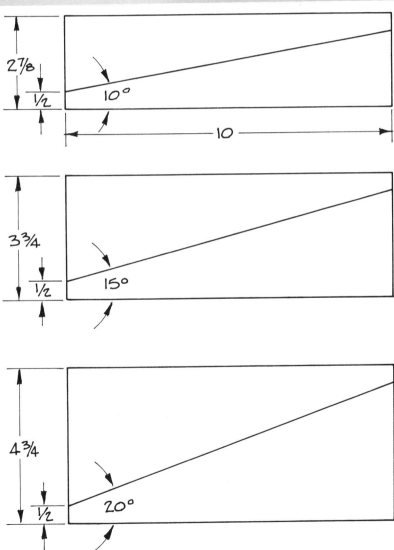

Illus. 5-3. A cutting diagram for making a set of angle blocks. Saw stock that is 2¼ inches thick.

2⅞

½

10°

10

3¾

½

15°

4¾

½

20°

Illus. 5-4. Angle blocks are used either singularly and/or in combination with other angle blocks, as shown here. When angle blocks are used one on top of each other, they are held together with dowel pins.

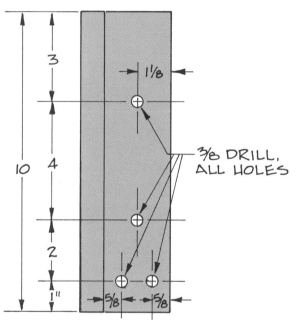

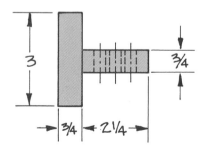

Illus. 5-5. This drilling guide (template) ensures that all holes on each block will be drilled alike at the same spacings so that they can be fitted together and used interchangeably with each other.

74

Chapter VI
Ring-Sanding Disc

High-quality bowls made with laminated rings require minimum glue lines that can only result from flat, perfectly mating surfaces. Carefully sanding the gluing surfaces makes the best true and flat glue joints. This operation is accomplished with a special ring-sanding disc used in a drill press. The drill-press-mounted sanding disc places the sanding operation on a horizontal plane. This allows you to bring the sanding surface lightly and uniformly to the abrasive from the bottom side of the disc, as shown in Illus. 6-1. Apply only minimal pressure to the abrasive, to prevent overheating that might induce warpage or distortion.

The components of the ring-sanding disc include one 9- and one 3¼-inch-diameter round disc sawn from ¾-inch-thick hardwood plywood. Mount a No. 4309 Disston Super Arbor, available at most hardware stores (Illus. 6-2 and 6-3), or a similar arbor.

Drill a 1¼-inch hole ¼ inch deep into the center of the small plywood disc for a recess for the head of the arbor. Then drill a ½-inch hole the rest of the way through the center of the disc. Attach the small plywood disc to the center of the 9-inch-diameter disc with three No. 10 × 1¼-inch wood screws. After assembly, check the ring-sanding disc to be sure it runs true. You may have to add a paper shim under one screw to make the sanding surface rotate on a perfectly true, horizontal plane. Paint the sand-

ing surface of the 9-inch-diameter disc with enamel to seal the wood and provide a working surface for the adhesive to hold the abrasive paper.

Use a sheet of 9 × 11-inch, 80-grit, 3-M Free Cut Production Paper (or a similar

Illus. 6-1. A drill-press-mounted disc sander being used to prepare the gluing surfaces of the rings.

75

Illus. 6-2. The sanding disc is made from two pieces of ¾-inch-thick hardwood plywood and a threaded arbor.

Illus. 6-3. Details for the ring-sanding disc, which consists of two ¾-inch thick hardwood plywood discs with diameters of 3¼ and 9 inches and a threaded arbor. Note that the flange and the nut of the threaded arbor are secured to the smaller wood disc which, in turn, is fastened to the larger one.

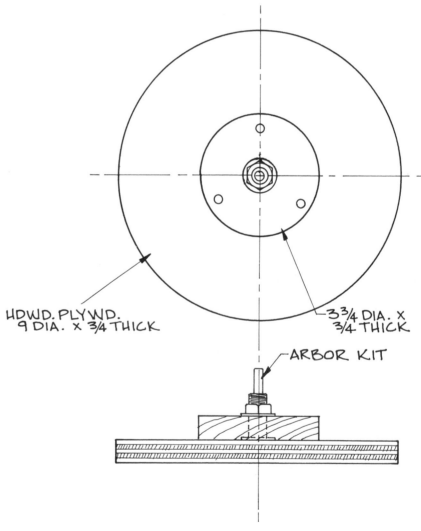

HDWD. PLYWD.
9 DIA. X ¾ THICK

3¾ DIA. X
¾ THICK

ARBOR KIT

product) for the abrasive. You can cut the abrasive to its round shape using the cutting board shown in Illus. 8-9 on page 86, or it can be trimmed with a knife after it is bonded to the plywood disc. Use No. 2, 3-M Feathering Disc Adhesive (or a similar contact cement) to bond the abrasive onto the plywood disc. This adhesive is available from paint departments of automotive supply stores.

Usually a coat of adhesive is applied to both the abrasive paper and the sander disc. Once the abrasive paper is applied, the disc is ready for sanding the gluing surfaces of the rings.

When making bowls that are larger than 9 inches in diameter, make a larger sanding disc. The abrasive paper will have to be cut from two sheets of paper and the edges carefully butted together on the disc.

Before sanding the rings, be sure to check that the register lines and the reference word *top* marked on the rings have been extended to the sides or the bevel-sawn surfaces of the rings. Sanding the rings will remove the original registration lines, which would pose a problem subsequently with the grain alignment if you did not extend the reference marks. Illus. 6-1 shows the ring-sanding operation.

Sand all mating surfaces, as well as the top of the top ring and the bottom of the base. This ensures that equal pressure will be applied to all the surfaces during gluing. When sanding, exert more pressure on higher or thicker areas than on lower areas.

The recommended speed of the sanding disc in the drill press is about 1200 rpm. Begin sanding the ring by holding it against the sanding disc with very light pressure. Remove the ring, rotate it about a sixth of a turn, replace it, and sand it again: repeat this procedure until a full rotation has been made. You will be able to feel when the ring's gluing surface is flat and smooth.

Check the fit of the rings with a light, as shown in Illus. 6-4. Holding the assembled bowl against the light with your hands will reveal open joints and if any additional sanding is needed.

As soon as you are satisfied that the mating surfaces are all tight, glue the bowl. This will minimize any dimensional distortion that might occur from a change in humidity.

Vacuum away the dust from the ring and base components before gluing them together, this ensures that you will apply the glue to a clean surface. Instructions for the gluing operation are given in Chapter VII.

Illus. 6-4. Check the fit of the rings with a light source.

77

Chapter VII
Bowl-Gluing Press

The individual rings glued together to form the bowl must be clamped with sufficient pressure and squarely, without shifting, while the glue sets. Brick or block weights will work, but the shop-made bowl-gluing press described here is more helpful (Illus. 7-1 and 7-2). It is also portable, so it can be moved out of the way while other work is in progress.

The bowl-gluing press detailed in Illus. 7-3 is simple to make and meets all the necessary requirements. It is a small press that will accommodate bowls up to 8 inches in diameter. Simply increasing the diameter of

Illus. 7-2. Bowl presses can be made of any size to accommodate large and deep bowls.

Illus. 7-1. A typical bowl-gluing press.

the two plywood discs is all that is necessary to make a larger press. Here is the list of materials needed for the small press:

    A. Two pieces of ¾-inch-thick plywood, 10 inches in diameter.

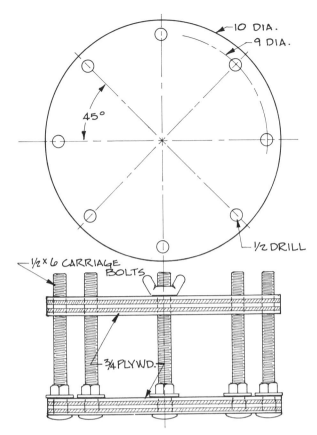

Illus. 7-3. Details for making a small bowl-gluing press.

B. Eight ½- × 6-inch fully threaded carriage bolts. (½-inch redi-bolt, which is a continuously threaded rod, can be cut and used instead of bolts to handle any required vertical opening.)
C. Eight ½-inch NC nuts
D. Eight ½-inch flat washers (16 nuts and washers if using a redi-bolt)
E. Eight ½-inch wing nuts

MAKING THE BOWL-GLUING PRESS

Scribe 10-inch circles on both pieces of plywood, and a 9-inch circle on one piece for drilling the bolt holes. Mark the locations of the bolt holes 45-degrees apart. Saw out the 10-inch-diameter discs. Clamp the two pieces of plywood together. Mark registration lines across the edges of the two discs for alignment and assemble them according to the way they were drilled. Drill ½-inch holes through the two plywood discs with one on top of the other.

Use a piece of small dowel and sandpaper to enlarge the holes in the top piece, to facilitate easy assembly and removal of the bowl from the press.

A dab of paint on the end of one bolt and around the corresponding hole in the top piece can serve as registration marks for the assembly, making it easier to use.

Cut two 9-inch-diameter pieces of plastic film to put under and above the bowl for protection against accidental gluing of the bowl to the press.

Before gluing, make sure that the register lines and the word *top* are clearly marked on the outside edges of the rings and base. If they are not marked, you may be able to go back to the pattern drawing and transfer them to the wood. The word *top* is usually marked at the point where the angular drilling hole is made for cutting out the inside of the ring. Also, before gluing make sure that all of the gluing surfaces have been sanded and checked.

Plastic resin glue (Illus. 7-4) is a good type of glue to use. It is a powder that is mixed with water. Plastic resin glue sets chemically and is highly resistant to water. Only a small quantity of glue is needed for a bowl. It is easy to mix, and can be cleaned up with soap and water before it sets.

Begin the gluing operation by placing a piece of plastic on the bottom surface of the gluing press. Coat the top edge (gluing surface) of the base piece and set it in the press with the word *top* visible between two of the

Illus. 7-4. Gluing a bowl. Note the slight but uniform squeeze-out of glue that indicates it has been adequately spread. Also note the plastic between the bowl and the bottom of the press; this plastic ensures that the bowl does not inadvertently become glued to the press.

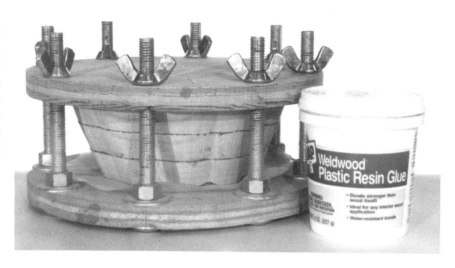

bolts. Now, coat the top and bottom surfaces of the next ring, then place the ring on the base piece with the word *top* and the register lines aligned. Continue coating the rest of the rings with glue in the same manner. Remember, it will *not* be necessary to add a coat of glue to the top of the top ring. Set the piece of protective plastic over the top ring and position the top of the press in place.

Turn the wing nuts snug to the top piece, but do not use excessive pressure. Then tighten every third wing nut about a quar-

ter turn until the pressure feels even on all the bolts, and then tighten each wing nut about a quarter turn more (Illus. 7-1). The excess glue being squeezed out of the joints will indicate that the joints are tight.

Check to see that the word *top* and the register lines are all properly aligned and that no pieces have shifted. If necessary, release the pressure, realign the rings, and reapply the pressure.

After the glue sets (usually overnight), remove the bowl from the press. You are now ready to finish-shape and sand the bowl.

Chapter VIII
Sanding Balls

Shop-made sanding balls (Illus. 8-1) are the key to the stacked-ring bowl-making process. Sanding balls solve two major important problems involved in bowl-making. First, they provide a means to do the final shaping of the inside contours. Second, they are used to smooth-sand the inside spherical surfaces of the bowl. The balls are easy to make, and can be made with basic tools found in most home workshops.

Sanding balls will also have many uses in other woodworking activities. There is nothing commercially available exactly like them to shape and smooth wood. This chapter gives complete, detailed step-by-step procedures for making sanding balls covered with coarse-cloth-backed abrasives or with finer-grit, paper-backed abrasives.

Commercially available sponge-rubber balls sold in toy stores have the perfect resilience and size requirements to support the abrasives. One commonly available brand—the Super Pinky ball—is firm, but still soft enough to have the necessary flexibility (Illus. 8-2). This is an ideal ball, and appears to be a standard in the toy industry. Other brands of sponge rubber balls that are the same size as the Super Pinky are available. It is advisable to make at least four sanding balls at once, each with different abrasive grits: 36, 120, 240, and 320.

BALL-CUTTING JIG

To begin making a sanding ball, first cut a segment off the sponge-rubber ball, to give it a flat surface so that it can be mounted onto the spindle (Illus. 8-3). As a safety precaution, quickly make a holder for this cutting job, as detailed in Illus. 8-4. The holder is made of two pieces of ¾ × 2½ × 4-inch plywood glued together. Scribe a 2⅜-inch

Illus. 8-1. The three sanding balls on the right are sponge-rubber balls that are covered with abrasives of various grits. At left is a piece of cloth-backed, 36-grit abrasive that is cut out so that it will wrap uniformly over the surfaces of the ball.

Illus. 8-2. Use inexpensive rubber balls available from most toy stores to make your own arbor-mounted sanding balls.

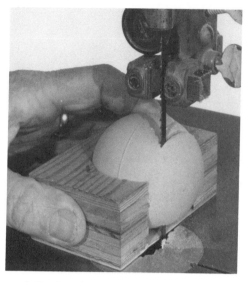

Illus. 8-3. Cutting a flat surface on a sponge-rubber ball with a band saw. This can be done safely if you use a simple shop-made holder.

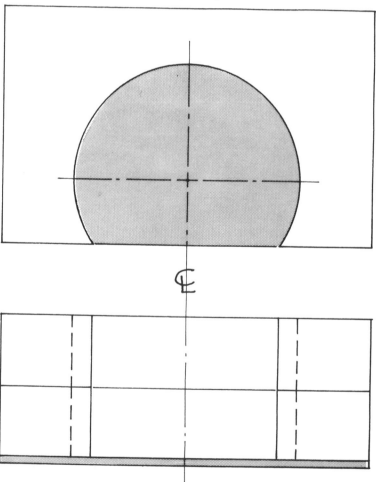

Illus. 8-4. A full-size plan for making a ball-cutting jig. The top view is shown above the front view.

82

circle in the center of the 4-inch side, $^{11}/_{16}$ inch from the edge; this circle will be used as a center point. Saw out the circle, cutting just inside the line; because you are cutting just inside the line, you will have to compress the ball slightly to fit it into the holder. Glue a piece of veneer or thin wood to the bottom of the holder to complete it.

Saw the ball off so that the line of cut is flush with the edge of the holder, as shown in Illus. 8-3.

BALL SPINDLE

The spindle parts of the sanding ball consist of a $^5/_{16} \times 5$-inch carriage bolt (with the threads cut off) and a piece of $^3/_4$-inch-thick pine wood (Illus. 8-5 and 8-6). Scribe a 2-inch-diameter circle on the pine wood. Using a $^3/_4$-inch spade bit, bore a hole in the center of the circle, $^3/_{16}$ inch deep.

Now, drill a $^5/_{16}$-inch hole completely through the center. With the scroll-saw table set to 15 degrees, bevel-cut the circle so that the bottom will have a smaller diameter than the top (Illus. 8-5). Either add epoxy to the bolt head or 3M Black Super Weatherstrip Adhesive, part #08008 (available in the paint department of automotive supply stores), to the wood piece; then drive the square head of the bolt into the pine so that it is flush with the top. The square under the head of the bolt prevents it from turning in the wood.

Coat the flat surface of the ball and the top side of the assembled wood piece with 3M Black Super Weatherstrip Adhesive, and allow them to dry. Do this about an hour before you're ready to glue the ball to the wood of the spindle.

Illus. 8-5 (right). This drawing shows the relationship of the bevelled wood block to the "flat" on the sponge rubber ball.

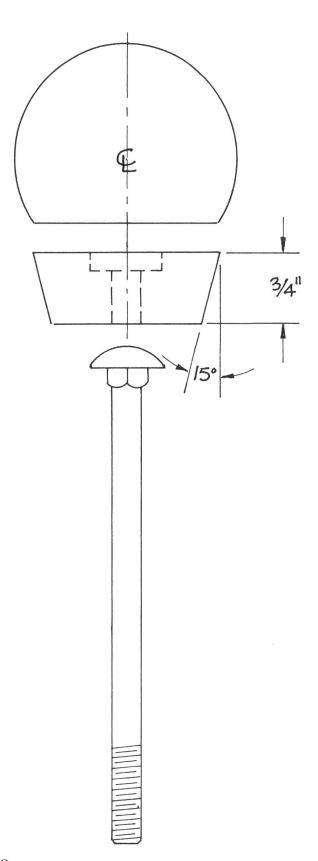

CLAMP

The clamp used to assemble the sanding balls to the spindle (Illus. 8-6) is very important because the sanding balls must run true on the spindle, without wobbling, to work properly. The clamp consists of two pieces of 1 × 4 × 4-inch hardwood, two ⁵⁄₁₆-inch full-threaded carriage bolts, six ⁵⁄₁₆-inch NC nuts, two ⁵⁄₁₆-inch wing nuts, and one piece of ³⁄₁₆ × 1 × 4-inch cold rolled steel. Illus. 8-7 gives all the details for making the clamp.

To make the clamp, begin by marking a point at the center of one block. Mark two points 1⅝-inch in on each side of this center for the bolt holes. Clamp the two blocks together for drilling; the drilling should be done on a drill press, so the holes are drilled at right angles to the blocks. Drill the two ⁵⁄₁₆-inch bolt holes through both pieces at the same time. Carefully cut the 2⅜-inch hole in the top piece; make sure that its center is exactly aligned with the ⁵⁄₁₆-inch hole for the spindle.

To assemble the ball to the spindle, coat the flat surface of the ball and the top of the bevelled pine piece with 3M Black Super Weatherstrip Adhesive. Allow it to dry, then apply a second coat of the Black Weatherstrip Adhesive to the ball's flat surface.

Place the ball and the carriage-bolt spindle assembly in the clamp. With the metal strip installed and the wing nuts tightened, set the unit aside until the adhesive has hardened, which takes about a half hour.

After removing the ball and spindle assembly from the clamp, drill a ⁵⁄₆₄-inch hole into the center of the ball. This hole will be used later to center the cut sheet of sanding abrasives onto the ball. To find the exact center of the ball, install the spindle in a drill or lathe and mark the ball's center with a soft pencil while it is rotating. Remove it and drill the hole.

Now the abrasives can be applied to the surfaces of the sanding balls. First cut the abrasives into circular or disc shapes. Then cut or slit these sheet abrasives so they conform to the contour of the ball (Illus. 8-8). A special shop-made cutting tool and a cutting board simplify this task; these aids also can be used to cut the initial round discs.

ABRASIVE-CUTTING SYSTEM

The shop-made sanding-disc cutter system is comprised of a cutting tool, a board, and two short dowel center stops. (Illus. 8-9–8-11). Using this system makes it easy

84

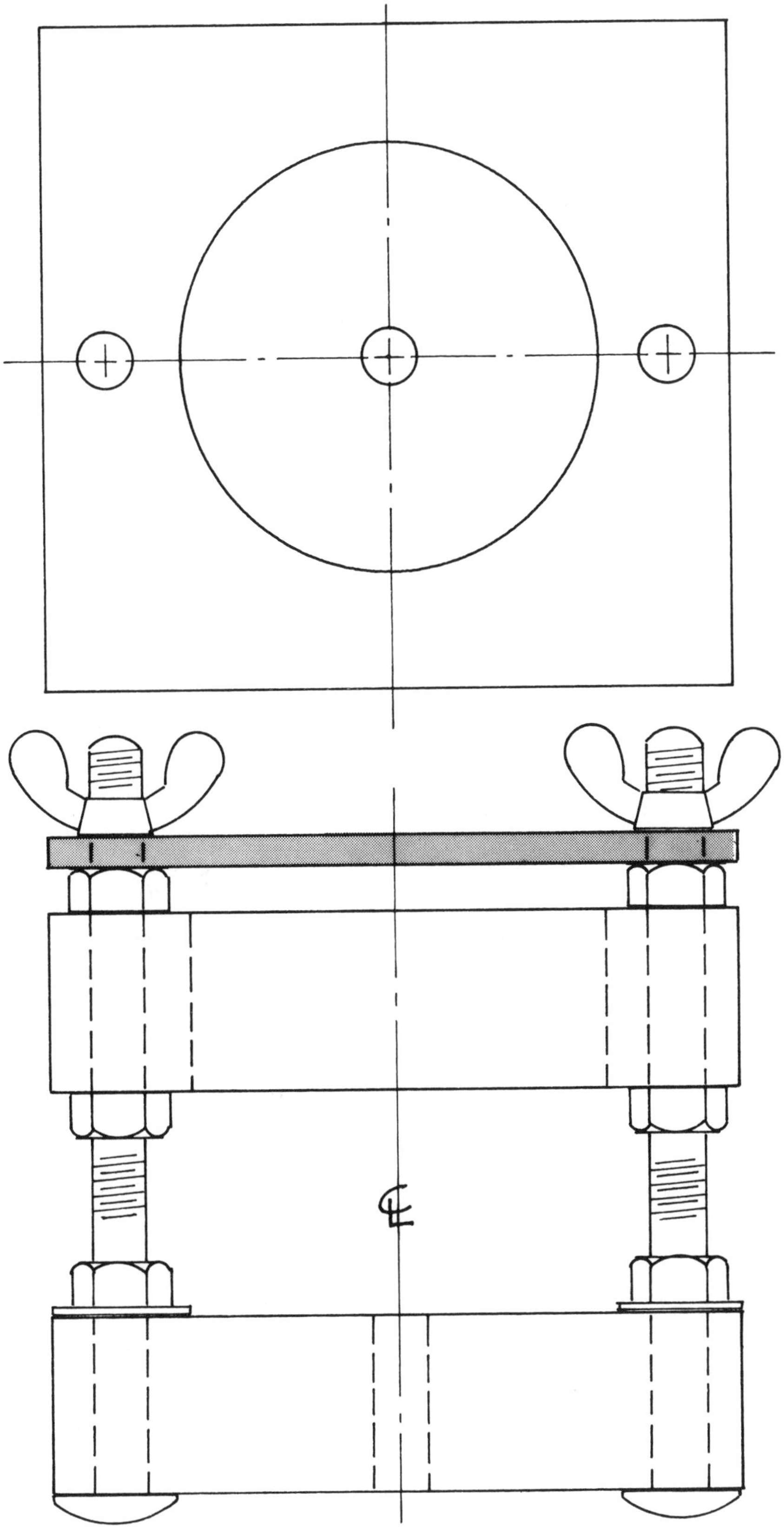

Illus. 8-7. A full-size drawing of the clamp used to assemble the sanding balls to the spindle.

to cut perfectly uniform abrasives each time. The cutter is designed so that it provides a good hand grip for cutting the heavy cloth-backed abrasive material. Finer-grit sandpaper discs can also be easily cut.

Illus. 8-10 provides a full-size drawing for making the cutting tool. Use a hardwood. Illus. 8-10 shows ⅞-inch-thick material, but slightly thicker material can be used.

Cut the outside shape of the cutter according to Illus. 8-10. Drill 1-inch holes at the ends of the hole for the hand grip, and cut out the material in between with a scroll saw. Using a ⅜-inch corner-rounding bit in a router, round off both sides around the hand hole and around the top and the non-cutting end.

The cutter is a No. 19 X-Acto blade. It is held in place with three #4 × ½-inch pan-head sheet-metal screws. The cutting edge is mounted far enough below the cutter so that the cutting edge can be resharpened with a whetstone when it gets dull.

Five ⁵⁄₆₄-inch pivot holes are drilled into the bottom of the cutter. Each is used for certain cutting operations. The holes are drilled on a line parallel to the side of the cutter and in line with the longest point of

Illus. 8-8. Simply slit the finer-grit abrasives, as shown at the left, to fit over the ball, but cut the coarse 36-grit abrasives to the "finger" shapes, as shown on the right.

Illus. 8-9. The components of the shop-made disc-abrasive-cutting system consist of a cutting tool, a board, and two dowel center stops. Note the metal inset (indicated by the pencil) set into the board. This helps to position or locate successive cuts without the need for measuring.

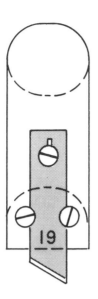

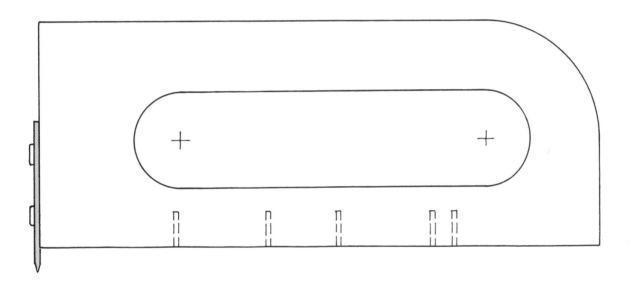

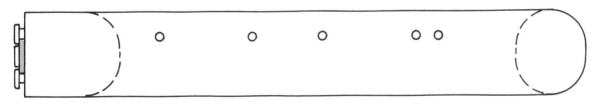

BOTTOM VIEW

Illus. 8-10. Full-size details for making the abra-
sive-cutting tool.

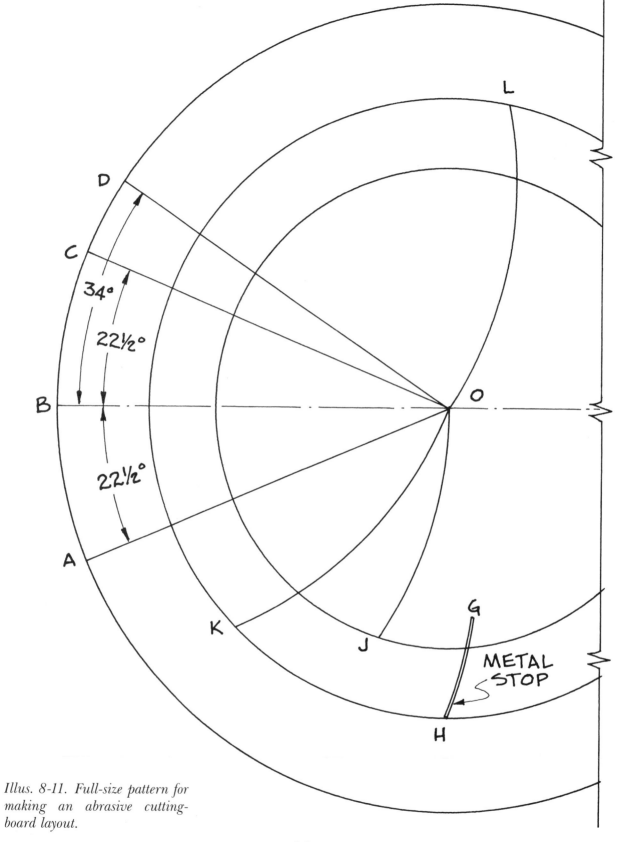

Illus. 8-11. Full-size pattern for making an abrasive cutting-board layout.

the cutter blade. Drill the holes 1½, 2½, 3¼, 4¼, and 4½ inches from the cutting edge.

The holes 1½ and 2½ inches from the cutting edge are used for cutting 3- and 5-inch-diameter abrasive sheets from 36-grit, cloth-backed abrasive material; this abrasive material is used with the 3- and 5-inch flat sanding discs used to sand convex surfaces. The hole 3¼ inches from the cutting edge is used to cut the 36-grit cloth-backed abrasive material that will be used on the sanding-balls' abrasive. The hole 4¼ inches from the cutting edge is used to cut the final "finger" shapes on the 36-grit cloth-backed abrasives for the sanding balls.

You will have to make special pattern cuts to the cloth-backed and sandpaper abrasives so that they will fit neatly on the surface of the sanding balls. The cutting board is designed to make these cuts by providing specific pivot points to the cutting tool (Illus. 8-9 and 8-11).

The cutting board is 8¾ inches square and is made of either a piece of sink cutout with a laminate covering or ¾-inch-thick plywood with a piece of laminate applied to it. The laminate provides a hard cutting surface that can withstand the many cuts that will be made on it.

Illus. 8-11 gives the full-size pattern for making an abrasive cutting-board layout. Mark all the pivot points and center with a punch or awl for drilling. Drill all the marked points with a ⁵⁄₆₄-inch drill.

Two 4d finish nails are used for pivot points. To lay out the metal stop, put a nail in hole A and, using the 4¼-inch-distance hole in the disc cutter, scribe a line between G and H. Using a #7 blade in a scroll saw, saw the scribed line between G and H. Cut a piece of 26-gauge, ¹⁵⁄₁₆ × 1⅛-inch sheet metal, smooth the edges, and shape it to fit into the saw cut made between G and H.

Inset it into the slot. This functions as a guide or stop that locates where successive cuts are to be made.

Two dowel-cutter center stops (Illus. 8-9) are needed for use with the cutting board. One is ½ inch in diameter by ¾ inch long, and the other is ⅞ inch in diameter and ¾ inch long. Both have a ⁵⁄₆₄-inch hole drilled vertically into their centers.

CUTTING CLOTH-BACKED ABRASIVES

The abrasives used in making the sanding balls are cut in special ways, so that they will conform to the surfaces of the ball. Two different patterns of cuts are used. The coarse, 36-grit cloth-backed abrasives are cut into circular discs first (Illus. 8-12) and then into a "finger" pattern (Illus. 8-13).

Illus. 8-12. Cutting a 6 × 48-inch, 36-grit cloth-backed abrasive belt into circular discs. The 3¼-inch-distance hole in the cutter handle is used with the nail-pivot point. The result will be a 6½-inch-diameter disc with two flat areas on its circumference.

89

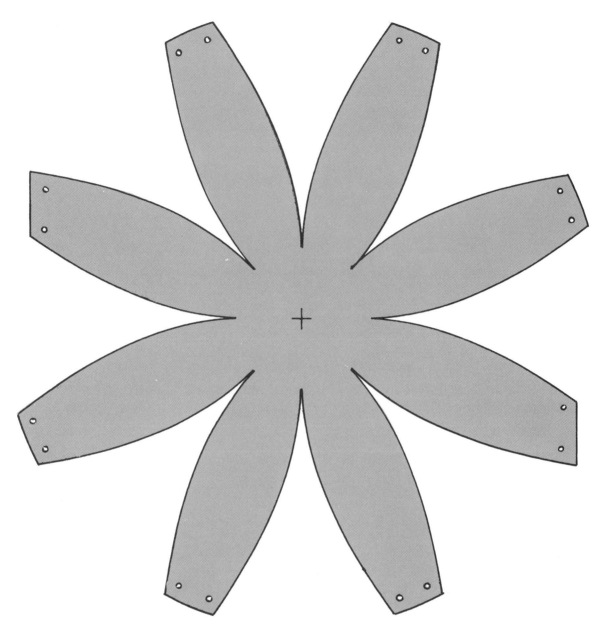

Illus. 8-13. The "fingers" pattern for 36-grit cloth-backed abrasive as cut from the 6½-inch-diameter disc. Note the angular ends on two of the "fingers" *(at 10 and 4 o'clock). This is due to material shortage that results from cutting a 6½-inch-diameter disc from a belt that is only 6 inches wide.*

The finer paper-backed abrasives are cut into patterned slits (Illus. 8-8). The ready-to-cut circular discs can be purchased as 5-inch-diameter, 120-, 240-, and 320-grit 3M Gold or Free Cut paper-sanding discs.

A cloth-backed, 36-grit 6 × 48-inch abrasive sanding belt is one abrasive material that is readily available for woodworkers. The 3- and 5-inch discs used for flat sanding discs and the 6½-inch disc used to cover the sanding balls can all be cut from this material. Cut all abrasives with the abrasives centered on the cutting board, and with their "backing" sides up.

Cutting a 6½-inch-diameter disc from a 6-inch wide belt sounds impossible, but it can be done. The disc, however, will have two flats, and two of the "fingers" will have an angular end, as shown in Illus. 8-13. The holes on the end of the fingers are made with a scratch awl; these holes are used for nailing the ends of the "fingers" to the circular wood disc attached to the end of the sanding-ball spindle.

To make the 6½-inch-diameter cloth-backed disc, open up a 6 × 48-inch endless abrasive belt by cutting across the middle of the splice. Make a hole with a scratch awl in the middle of the belt, and about 3¾ inches from the cut end. With the abrasive side towards the cutting board, put the hole over the 4d nail in the center of the cutting board. Set the cutting handle over the nail at the 3¼-inch-distance hole in the cutter handle. Make a circular cut to produce a 6½-inch-diameter disc with two flats on it, from the belt.

Remove the cutter handle from the center nail. Set the ⅞-inch-diameter dowel center stop over the center nail on top of the 6½-inch-diameter abrasive disc. Insert an-other 4d nail into the hole marked C on the cutting board. Set the cutting tool onto this nail 4¼ inches from the cutting blade. Rotate the abrasive disc to the point where the flat and the curved edges of the disc meet at point K of the cutting board. This is shown at the pencil point in Illus. 8-14. Make the cut from the center outward to the edge of the disc, as is also shown in Illus. 8-14. This may require an extra pass or two to complete the cut.

Rotate the disc counterclockwise and place the previously cut slit over the curved metal stop. Make the next cut, repeating the operation until all eight cuts have been made. This results in one side of each finger being cut (Illus. 8-15).

Move the nail from hole C to D and remove the ⅞-inch dowel center stop from the center nail. Place the disc-cutting tool so that its hole is 4¼ inches from the cutting edge over the nail at D. One of the cut slits of the disc should cradle the metal stop.

Now, cut from the outside inward to complete the remaining cuts for each "finger." After a few cuts are made, it will be necessary to hold the abrasive "finger" against the metal stop, as shown in Illus. 8-16, so that the last few cuts can be properly located.

Illus. 8-14. Starting to make the "finger" cuts on the heavy cloth-backed abrasive. Note the ⅞-inch-diameter center stop placed over the center pivot nail. Another nail is set into hole C of the cutting board and into the 4¼-inch-distance hole of the cutter. Make the first cut so that it ends at point K. This should also be where a flat and the curved edge of the disc meet.

91

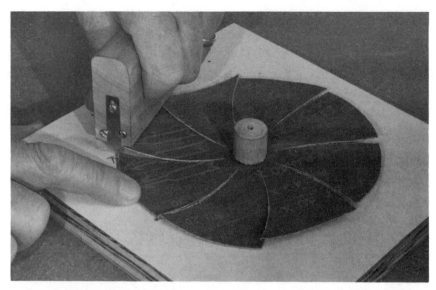

Illus. 8-15. The first eight cuts completed.

Illus. 8-16. Completing the remaining cuts of the "fingers." Work from the outside inward, and use the curved metal stop of the cutting board, as shown, to properly position the disc for each successive cut.

After cutting the cloth-backed discs, you should probably resharpen the blade of the disc cutter. A small whetstone does the job. A sharp cutter blade always works better.

CUTTING PAPER DISCS

Five-inch-diameter precut discs of paper-backed abrasives can be purchased from the paint department of automotive supply stores. 3M Gold 120-grit and 3M Free-Cut 240- and 320-grit discs are the best brands to use. These discs do not come with a hole in the center. However, you can cut a 5-inch hole-locating template from paper or from the plastic cover of a coffee can by using the disc-cutter tool and the cutting board. To punch a hole in the center of the abrasive disc, simply put the template on top of the abrasive disc and use a scratch awl, as shown in Illus. 8-17.

Insert a 4d nail in the hole at B of the cutting board and place a 5-inch-diameter abrasive disc over the center nail of the cutting board with the abrasive side down. Place the ½-inch-diameter dowel center stop on top of the 5-inch disc and over the

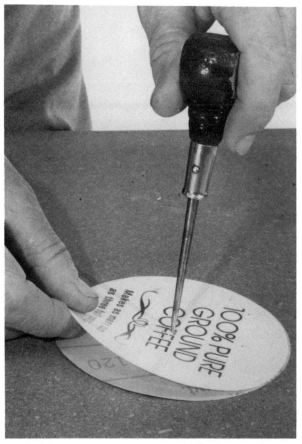

Illus. 8-17. Making a center hole in a precut abrasive disc with the aid of a circular plastic template and a scratch awl.

center nail of the cutting board. Set the disc-cutting tool's 4¼-inch-distance hole over the nail at B. Make the first cut on the disc, cutting from the center outward (Illus. 8-18).

Rotate the abrasive disc counterclockwise, and put the previously cut slit over the metal stop. Repeat until all 16 cuts have been made and you end up with a disc as shown in Illus. 8-19. All grits of the paper discs are cut in the same manner. After the disc has been cut, its paper side should look like it does in Illus. 8-19.

APPLYING ABRASIVES TO THE SANDING BALLS

The stiffness of the cloth-backed abrasive material does not allow it to conform easily to the shape of the ball. Consequently, each "finger" of the cut abrasive must be softened and shaped to fit the curvature of the ball. This is done by using a simple shaping block and a ball peen hammer, as shown in Illus. 8-20.

The block (Illus. 8-20–8-22) is made

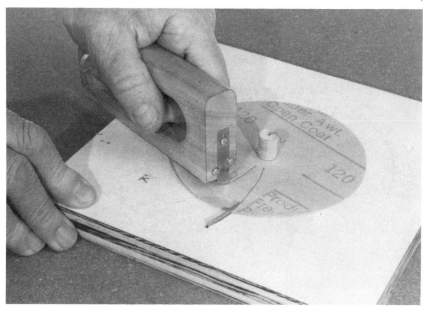

Illus. 8-18. Cutting slits into paper-backed abrasive discs. Note that the ½-inch-diameter dowel center stop is now in use.

Illus. 8-19. The final-cutting pattern for all paper-backed abrasives, including the 120-, 240-, and 320-grit discs.

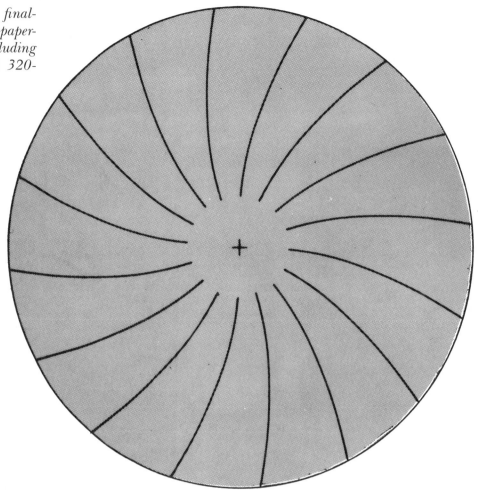

Illus. 8-20. Use a ball-peen hammer and the shop-made block shown here to shape each "finger" so it will fit the curve of the ball. This procedure is necessary only for the stiff, cloth-backed, 36-grit abrasives.

94

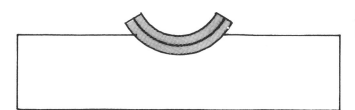

Illus. 8-21. A full-size end view of the shaping block shown in Illus. 8-20.

Illus. 8-22. A closer look at the simple forming block used to form the coarse-grit abrasive "fingers." A piece of rubber-backed carpet with its backing side up is tacked into a groove.

from a piece of ¾ × 3½ × 5-inch hardwood. A half-round groove ¹³⁄₁₆ inch wide and ³⁄₁₆ inch deep is cut lengthwise down the middle of the piece. You can cut this groove by using a cove-sawing technique on a table saw. Adjust the saw blade to make a ³⁄₁₆-inch-deep cut. Clamp a wood guide at a 17-degree angle to the blade and located so that the groove will be cut down the middle of the block. Lower the saw blade until it is almost flush with the saw table, and make the first cut. Continue to raise the saw blade a little at a time, and make successive cuts until the groove is ³⁄₁₆ inch deep.

Use a 1¼ × 5-inch piece of rubber-backed carpeting to line the groove; this carpeting is held in place by three small-headed nails. Place the carpet so that the rubber backing is up.

Shape the coarse-grit abrasive "fingers" with a small ball-peen hammer (Illus. 8-20). Use the hammer to lightly strike the cloth-backed side of each "finger" as it is held over the grooved shaping block. Start striking at the center, working back and forth and across and outward to form each "finger."

GLUING ABRASIVES TO THE SANDING BALLS

The abrasives are best held onto the sanding ball with 3M Feathering Disc Adhesive. This product comes in 5-ounce tubes and is available at the paint department of automotive supply stores. There are two types of this adhesive: one is number 08041 Feathering Disc Adhesive, and the other is number 08051. The first type is more permanent and should be used only for mounting cloth-backed abrasives to rubber balls. Number 08051 Feathering Disc Adhesive is used for mounting paper-backed abrasives.

Coarse Cloth-Backed Abrasive Balls

Apply the adhesive to the ball and spread it over the surface using a piece of used abrasive paper, as shown in Illus. 8-23 and 8-24. Use a 5-inch-diameter piece of ¾-inch-thick plywood with a 4d nail in the center to hold both cloth- and paper-backed abrasives. Apply the same 3M Feathering Disc

Illus. 8-23. Applying 3M Feathering Disc Adhesive to the surfaces of the sponge rubber ball.

Illus. 8-24. Quickly spread the adhesive evenly with a piece of used abrasive paper or cardboard, as shown.

Adhesive to all the fingers of the cloth-backed abrasive, and spread it evenly (Illus. 8-25 and 8-26).

With the adhesive applied, and the abrasive still on the holder, carefully bring the abrasive to the surface of the ball. To position the abrasive for initial contact, simply push the nail of the holder into the hole in the center of the ball. This will automatically center the abrasive on the ball (Illus. 8-27). Press each "finger" down on the wooden base of the ball (Illus. 8-28).

Secure the ends of each finger with two #17 × ¾-inch-headed wire nails (Illus. 8-29). This is done to prevent the abrasive from twisting on the ball, due to the drag on it when you rough-out the bowl.

Illus. 8-25. The feathering adhesive is also applied to the back of the abrasive.

96

Illus. 8-26. Spreading out the cement as evenly as possible.

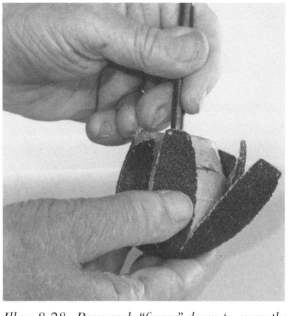

Illus. 8-28. Press each "finger" down to cover the surface of the sponge ball.

Illus. 8-27. Positioning the cut and cement-applied abrasive on the ball. The nail of this simple jig is pushed into a hole previously drilled into the end of the ball; this automatically centers the abrasive.

Illus. 8-29. Nailing the "finger" ends completes the job of making a coarse, 36-grit abrasive ball.

Fine Paper-Backed Abrasive Balls

Cover the finer-grit, 5-inch-diameter paper-backed abrasives with the feathering disc adhesive. Also apply the feathering disc adhesive to the surface of the ball, as was done for the cloth-back abrasive balls (Illus. 8-23–8-26 and 8-30). Use the holder to position the abrasive on the ball, centering it perfectly as shown in Illus. 8-31. Push the abrasive firmly against the ball, and then remove it from the holder.

Illus. 8-30. Spreading out the cement on a paper-backed abrasive disc.

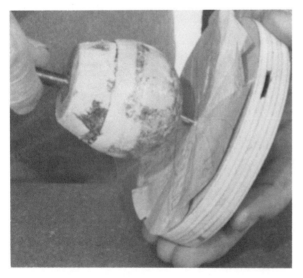

Illus. 8-31. The nail of the holder is used to center the abrasive to the ball.

To press the abrasive segments onto the ball, hold the ball so that the spindle is pointing away from you. Press down only the counterclockwise edge of the first segment, as shown in Illus. 8-32. The clockwise edge must remain up, so that the edge of

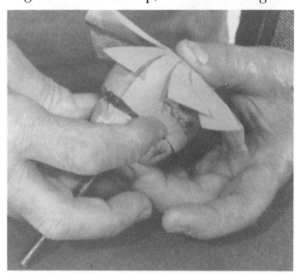

Illus. 8-32. Holding the ball as shown (from the operator's view), press just the left-hand edge of the first abrasive segment to the ball. The right-hand edge must be left up, so that the final segment can be inserted under it.

the last segment can be slipped under it. After the first segment is in place, smooth each segment down; work from the center of the ball outwards and counterclockwise around the entire sanding ball (Illus. 8-33). Slip the edge of the last segment under the edge of the first, as shown in Illus. 8-34. Illus. 8-35 shows a completed sanding ball with fine-grit abrasive applied to it.

Finally, use a strong rubber band (one used for broccoli in supermarkets is ideal) to hold the edges in place (Illus. 8-1).

Worn abrasives can be stripped and replaced without much difficulty. After making a few bowls, you will find it convenient to have two or three sanding balls of each grit ready so that you don't have to stop to change abrasives.

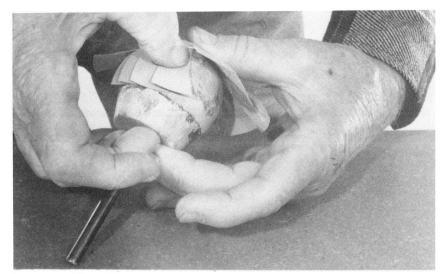

Illus. 8-33. Press down the "fingers" or segments of the abrasive one at a time, working from the center outward and counterclockwise around the ball.

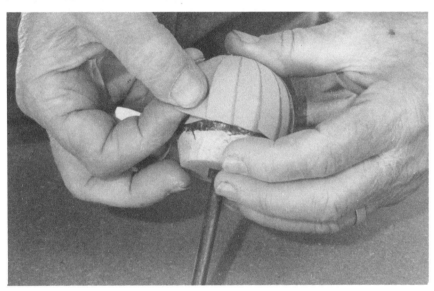

Illus. 8-34. Slipping the edge of the final segment under the first segment.

Illus. 8-35. The completed ball ready for use. The paper will conform completely to the shape of the sanding ball as soon as sanding begins.

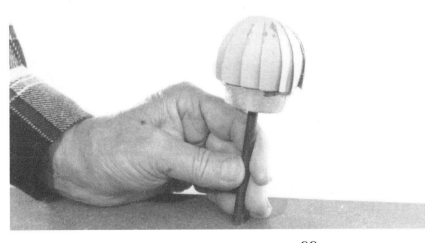

Chapter IX
Scalloped Edges and Fretwork Trim

You can dramatically enhance the overall appearance of a simple bowl by forming a continuously scalloped design around the top edge of the bowl. Although any design of repeating circular segments will add a special touch to an otherwise plain bowl, combining a scalloped edge with complementary fretwork openings gives a very delicate and unusual look to a bowl.

However, always guard against adding too much ornamentation to a bowl. This can be counterproductive. A bowl with too much ornamentation can be as unappealing as a plain bowl. The key to a good bowl design is to carefully consider the form, color, and ornamentation that will complement each other. The shape of the bowl's top-view profile often suggests the most ap-

propriate top-edge scallop design ornamentation, if any is advantageous at all.

SCALLOPED EDGE

A bowl can have no scallop, a shallow scallop, or a deep scallop. Often, the bowl is best left with no scallop at all—that is, straight and untouched. A good example is shown in Illus. 9-1. The multiple-wood insert under the top ring of the bowl is essentially straight when viewed directly from the side. A scalloped edge on this bowl would clash with the straight-line look of the multicolored insert, which is the focal point of the bowl.

Illus. 9-2—9-4 show examples of scalloped

Illus. 9-1. A decorative, fluted bowl without a scalloped top edge. A scalloped edge would clash with the flat and straight geometrical look of the multi-wood inset (inlay).

Illus. 9-2. This fluted bowl looks best with a slight scalloped edge that corresponds to the general top-view shape of the bowl.

Illus. 9-3. The top-view design of this bowl has large and small flutes and the scallop design has large and small projecting segments.

Illus. 9-4. This large, 12-inch-diameter fluted salad bowl looks good with a minor scalloped edge of minimal deflection.

edge designs that are a shallow deflection from a straight line around the top of the bowl. In general, the scallop line should not deviate drastically from the top-view outline of the bowl. However, Illus. 9-5 shows a deeply scalloped edge on a bubinga fruit bowl that is resting on a raised base. In this instance, a deeply scalloped edge seems to enrich the overall look.

The final determination of exactly what scallop design, if any at all, should be given to the top edge depends entirely upon the preference of the bowl maker and/or the wishes of the party(s) that may purchase or eventually own the bowl.

FRETWORK TRIM

Fretted work around the upper walls of a bowl gives the bowl a more interesting appearance. Fretted designs look best on bowls that are made from one basic, mono-colored wood (Illus. 9-6–9-8).

Cut the fretted openings on the scroll saw

Illus. 9-5. An example of a major or deeply scalloped edge.

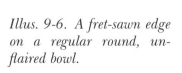

Illus. 9-6. A fret-sawn edge on a regular round, un-flaired bowl.

Illus. 9-7. Another regular round bowl that was made in the usual manner before the fretwork design was sawn.

Illus. 9-8. A fretted design has been cut into this bulbous bowl.

(Illus. 9-9). This work is best done to round or oval unflaired bowls, rather than fluted or lobed bows. The latter are more difficult to support flatly on the saw and, because of the short grains created by their shapes, they are more likely to tear and chip along the saw cuts.

Any number of beautiful fret designs can be developed, from simple multiple-heart patterns to complex geometric patterns. Fret patterns can be sawn on regular bowls (Illus. 9-6 and 9-7) and also on bulbous bowls, as shown in Illus. 9-8. The procedures are only slightly different.

A fret-sawn regular bowl is made and glued up completely as a single unit in the usual manner. It is worked close to its final shape before the fretwork design is sawed and applied. A bulbous fretwork bowl has inward, returning walls; therefore, the upper rings of this type of bowl must be cut through before they are glued to the rest of the bowl assembly (Illus. 9-9 and 9-10).

Bulbous fretted bowls are prepared in

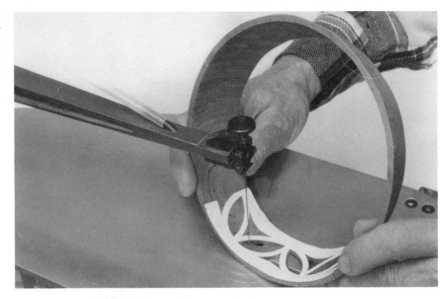

Illus. 9-9. Sawing a fretted pattern that covers an area of two pre-assembled rings for the top of the bulbous bowl shown in Illus. 9-8.

Illus. 9-10. When the fret-work is completed, the two sections are glued together.

two sections; the sections are glued together after the designs are sawn out. The two top rings are glued together to comprise the one fret-sawn upper half of the bowl.

Patterns

Illus. 9-11 gives full-size quarter patterns for fluted bowls 7½ inches in diameter. Four copies of the particular design are required, so that the design goes entirely around the inside of the bowl. Glue the pattern(s) to the inside walls of the bowl with 3M Temporary Bond Spray Mount Artist's Adhesive, No. 6065 (Illus. 9-12), or use rubber cement. In either case, apply just a light coating of adhesive to the back of the paper pattern. Do not apply adhesive directly to the wood.

Note that the ends of the patterns given in Illus. 9-11 run directly through the centers of their repeating designs. Minor adjustments can be made in the layout and sawing to compensate for slight variations in the bowl size. The ends of the patterns should correspond to the original registration lines used to make the bowl.

Once the patterns are in place, carefully

Illus. 9-11. Quarter patterns for fretted bowls 7½ inches in diameter. Note: Make slits in the patterns at lines A and B in the second ring area so that the patterns will conform to the three-dimensional shape of the inside surfaces resulting from these two rings being cut at different angles.

105

Illus. 9-12. The top and bottom sections on this bulbous bowl have been made separately. This facilitates the sawing of the fretwork designs, which must be sawn before final assembly because of the limitations of the scroll saw.

drill small saw-gate holes in all waste areas so you can thread the scroll-saw blade through the walls.

Fret-Sawing

Use a 2/0 scroll-saw fret blade (Illus. 9-9). It will make fine, smooth cuts and keep sanding to a minimum. You may want to experiment with spiral blades that have the advantage of sawing in any direction. Spiral blades do not produce cuts that are as smooth as the ones cut by regular fret-cutting blades. However, spiral blades may be the only possible choice when you are cutting certain patterns that you have designed and developed yourself.

When sawing the fretted openings in round bowls, you will quickly learn important techniques. For example, it is usually helpful to rough-out an area so there is room for the blade to be in a non-cutting position as you manipulate the work to begin a new cut or to complete another cut from a different direction. Also, you will note that it's impossible to cut out full circles in one continuous "sweep," as done in conventional sawing. You can only cut part of a circle at a time. Some lines parallel to the top edge are also difficult to cut. And it is always necessary to consider the sawing re-

strictions imposed by the scroll saw itself.

Occasionally, you may be confronted with a seemingly impossible cut. This situation can often be handled simply by installing the blade rearwards so that the teeth point to the rear of the machine. This type of cut takes some practice and concentration when feeding the wood. To saw accurately and maintain full control over the work, cut at a slow blade speed and follow the pattern lines carefully.

Sanding

Once all the fretwork sawing is completed, it is necessary to reduce the wall thickness in the fretwork area, to achieve the preferred delicate effect. Carefully use a sanding ball on the inside surfaces and a disc sander on the outside surfaces, as usual. Do *not* use any abrasives coarser than 120 grit from this point on. Coarse abrasives will tear and chip away "short grain" areas of the fretted design.

Finish-sand with 240-grit abrasive, followed with 320-grit abrasive. Slightly round all sharp sawn edges by hand with a folded piece of fine abrasive. The fretwork process in bowl work may take more work than expected. However, the results are unquestionably spectacular, and this should overshadow the time and effort involved.

Chapter X
Basic Inlays

The router's capability to make perfect inlays of almost any conceivable shape can be exploited to a high degree in this type of bowl work. Inlays are usually made from highly contrasting woods, so that the viewer's attention is drawn to them. In this chapter, just two types of many inlay possibilities are described and illustrated: the bottom inlay (Illus. 10-1), and the top-ring inlay (Illus. 10-2), which is most effective on bowls with flaired sides. These types of inlays can be used separately or in combinations, as shown in Illus. 10-2.

The items necessary for making the two kinds of inlays shown in this chapter include the following: a router (a plunging router is recommended), a ⁷⁄₁₆ outside-diameter template guide, an inlay bushing with a ¼-inch wall that fits over the template guide, and a ¼-inch flat-cutting bit. The router inlay kit shown in Illus. 10-3 is manufactured by Oak Park Enterprises Ltd., Box 13, Station A, Winnipeg, Manitoba, R3K 129 Canada. This one and similar ones that fit Porter Cable's ⁷⁄₁₆-inch template guide are available from major woodworking mail-order catalogues. Also needed is a template that you must make yourself. Make the template from ¼-inch-thick tempered hardboard, plywood, or plastic (Illus. 10-4).

The inlay must be designed and planned according to the shape and size desired. Review Chapter IV, which describes template-routing and the factors that will determine the size of the template.

There are two things to remember when making template-cut inlays. First, use the inlay bushing that fits over the template guide, and is held there by a small allen setscrew, *only* when routing the female recess. Second, remove the bushing from the template guide when you cut the male plug inlay. The same template is used for both operations.

When preparing the template, draw two register lines on both surfaces of the template. This is done because the inlay recess is cut with one side of the template placed up, and the plug inlay itself is cut with the other surface up.

Illus. 10-1. A typical bottom inlay of bird's-eye maple. Note that its shape corresponds to the overall top-view shape of the bowl.

Illus. 10-2. Bird's-eye maple with a bottom inlay and a top-ring inlay of purpleheart wood.

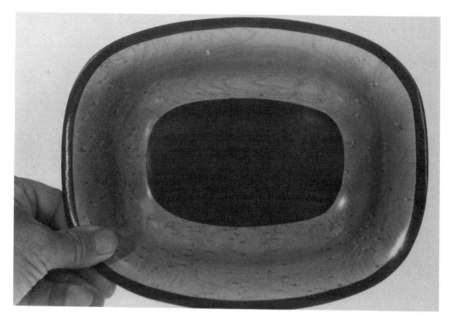

Illus. 10-3. Router accessories for basic inlay work consist of a template guide (at left), a ¼-inch inlay bushing (at right), and a ¼-inch-diameter router bit.

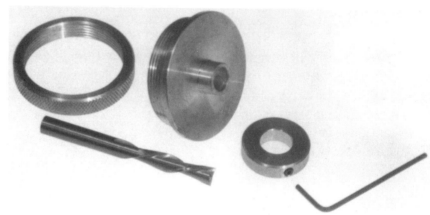

Illus. 10-4. Scroll-sawing a template from ¼-inch-thick hardboard.

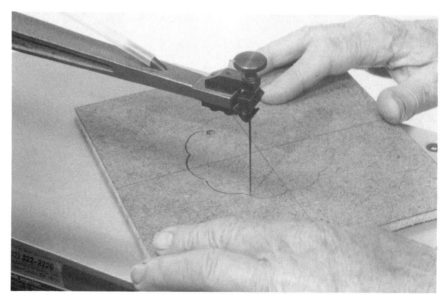

108

MAKING A BOTTOM INSIDE INLAY

Cut the bottom inlay recess to a depth of only about ⅛–³⁄₁₆ inch. Make this cut on the previously routed-out area that is typically made to rough-shape the bottom insides of all bowls (Illus. 10-5 and 10-6). Tack the template to the bowl blank at two opposite corners with two small headless brads. Make sure that the registration lines of the template are aligned with the registration lines marked on the bowl blank.

To cut the bottom inlay plug that fits into the recess, flip the template over and tack it to the inlay stock as shown in Illus. 10-7. When the template is flipped over, the upper surface of the inlay will come into contact with the bottom or the gluing surface of

Illus. 10-5. Tack the template to the bowl blank at opposite corners with brads after the routing out of the inside area has been completed.

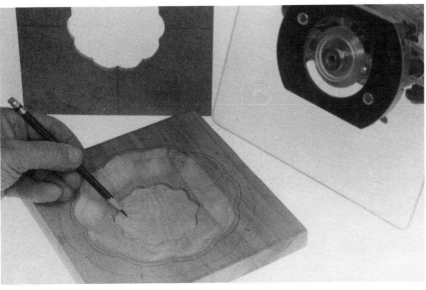

Illus. 10-6. Here the bottom inlay recess has been completely routed. Note that the inlay bushing is mounted to the router's template guide for this operation.

Illus. 10-7. The inlay insert material sized to shape with the same router bit, but without the inlay bushing. Note that the template is turned over for this operation.

the recess when the inlay is glued in. Outline the shape of the inlay plug to no more than a ¼-inch routing depth. You do not have to rout it completely through the template to free it from the surrounding wood.

Once the inlay profile is routed completely around the template at a sufficient depth, saw it free of the surrounding wood. Simply resaw it on a table saw or band saw. When the inlay is inserted, the rough, resawn surface of the inlay plug will be up (Illus. 10-8 and 10-9). This shows that the inlay has a good gluing surface, and the

rough, resawn surface will be smoothed during the subsequent ball-sanding operation on the inside of the bowl.

MAKING A TOP-RING TRIM INLAY

You can make a bowl with a contrasting wood trim around the outer edge of its flaired top ring by inlaying the entire thick bowl blank into another piece of thinner

Illus. 10-8. The inlay is ready to be glued into the recess routed into the inside bottom of the bowl blank.

110

Illus. 10-9. The finished inlay work is shown at right. The one template needed for this work is shown at the left. The bowl blank is now ready to be scroll-sawn into rings, as usual.

wood (the trim ring). Illus. 10-10–10-12 show such a bowl, made of fishtail oak and hard maple. Prepare a typical ¾-inch-thick bowl blank in the usual way, with the bottom routed out areas cut into both surfaces of the blank. Study the drawings in Illus. 10-13.

The trim ring stock should be about ⁵⁄₁₆ inch thick. Use a router to cut out the inside opening of the trim ring; when making this cut, use a template, with the ⁷⁄₁₆-inch template guide and the inlay bushing mounted over it.

To make the thicker inlay piece, which is the bowl-blank inlay plug, first rout a groove ¼ inch deep into the surface, as shown in Illus. 10-13. Cut this groove using

the same template, but with the inlay bushing removed from the router's template guide. Throughout this routing operation, be sure to keep the template guide in continuous contact with the inside edge of the template.

Cut the outside bevelled edge of the first ring to its size and shape with a scroll saw before gluing the trim ring in place. When the excess material is cut away, the groove becomes a rabbeted lip all around the bowl blank (inlay plug), as shown in Illus. 10-13. The maple trim ring will be glued onto this ledge, all around.

Now, cut the bevel on the inside of the top ring with a scroll saw, to free it, removing it, with the trim ring inlay, from the bowl

Illus. 10-10. Fishtail oak with a maple trim ring. The oak is actually inlaid into the maple when the blank is prepared.

111

blank. Cut out the remaining rings from the blank with a scroll saw in the usual manner. Then glue them together, and sand and finish them like the rings on other bowls, forming and sanding the top edge in the usual manner (Illus. 10-13).

Illus. 10-11. The top side of the bowl, showing the maple trim ring surrounding the oak. The next step is to cut away the excess material extending past the blank's edge with a scroll saw (or band saw), and to then begin cutting the rings.

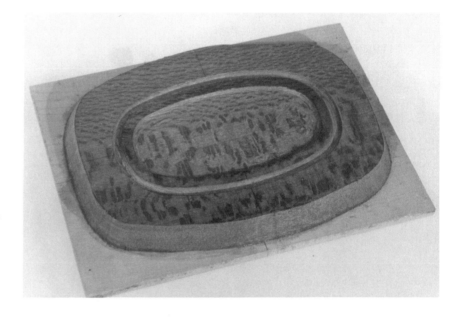

Illus. 10-12. The bottom view of the bowl. Note that the maple trim ring is only 5/16 inch thick. The exposed bowl edge was sawed to its initial bevelled shape before the trim ring was glued in place.

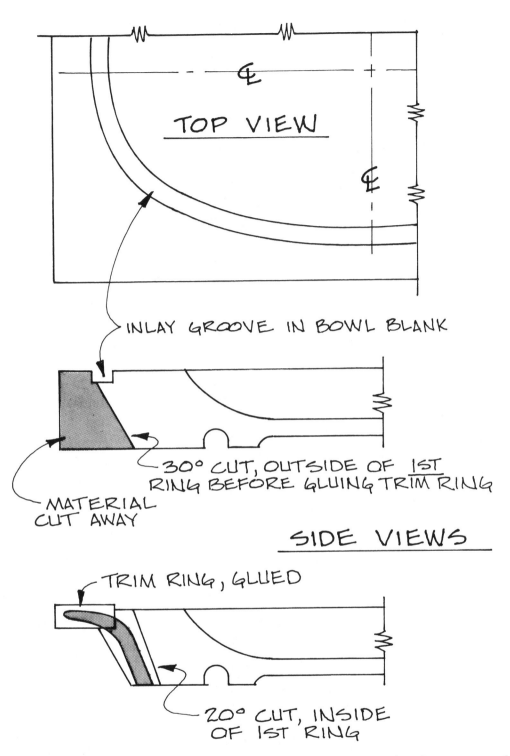

TOP VIEW

INLAY GROOVE IN BOWL BLANK

30° CUT, OUTSIDE OF 1ST
RING BEFORE GLUING TRIM RING

MATERIAL
CUT AWAY

SIDE VIEWS

TRIM RING, GLUED

20° CUT, INSIDE
OF 1ST RING

Illus. 10-13. Top- and side-view sketches showing the relationship of the bowl-blank inlay to the thin- *ner trim piece. Note that the router-cut edge of the inlay is bevel-sawn before being glued.*

113

Chapter XI
Decorative Inlays and Inserts

This chapter explores techniques in which contrasting wood inlays or inserts are glued into the bowl at different stages. In one technique, contrasting inlays are glued to just the top ring after it is cut out. This is considered a top-ring decoration. In other cases, the inlays or inserts are glued into the flat blank itself before the rings are sawn out. This forms a scalloped or wavy inlay effect. In those situations, the pattern develops out of the flat board. Another basic but effective technique is to simply glue various pieces between the layers of the rings. This is considered a multiple-wood insert technique.

These three basic techniques are explored below.

TOP-RING DECORATIONS

One easy and very effective technique is to glue evenly spaced square or round inlays, around the top ring (Illus. 11-1–11-3). Perfect circles will become ovals, and perfect squares will become diamond-shaped when the rings are bevel-cut. The shapes become even more pronounced or elongated the more the bowls are flaired. (Refer to the type B and C cross-sectional flaired shapes on pages 37 and 38.) This technique will also work with unflaired bowls (Illus. 11-3), but the oval and diamond shapes will not be as elongated as those shapes on a bowl with a full flair to its top ring.

Illus. 11-1. The drilled inlays on this top ring appear to be slightly oval due to the flair of the edge.

114

Illus. 11-2. Round brass tubing surrounds these wood dowel inlays.

Illus. 11-3. A mortising bit produces square holes which receive the square brass tubing that surrounds the square wood inlays.

The process is very simple. First, determine the number of holes or squares desired. Divide up the blank into that number of equal divisions (in degrees), and then lay out and mark the spacings on the bowl blank. Then drill round holes for the dowels on the blank with a sharp spur bit. Next, cut the square holes with a mortising bit to receive square inlay plugs (Illus. 11-4–11-6).

The procedure for sawing out the top ring is just slightly different. Cut the outside

of the top ring so that it has square edges; do not bevel-cut it until you have completed the drilling and gluing operations (Illus. 11-4 and 11-5). Cut the inside to a 20-degree bevel, as usual. However, do not make the inside secondary waste removal cut (for flaired bowls) until you have drilled and glued all the inserts.

Once the top ring is cut out, transfer the drilling location lines to the outside edge of the ring. Make the simple drill-press jig nec-

Illus. 11-4. At left is a typical ring after it has been drilled. At center are bowls with drilled and mortised inlays. Note the metallic tubing at the right.

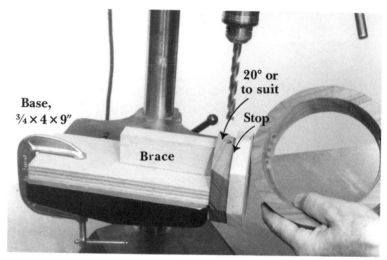

Illus. 11-5 (left). Drilling the top ring. Note that the outside edge of the ring is cut square at 90 degrees to make drilling easier. Later it is bevel-sawn so that it conforms to the appropriate flaired angle. Illus. 11-6 (above). The drill-press jig made for drilling round and square holes radially around the top ring.

essary to perform the radial drilling or mortising operation (Illus. 11-6). The work-supporting piece of the jig is cut at 20 degrees, and to match the inside diameter of the top ring. A stop which keeps all holes in a straight line is fastened to the curved and bevelled drilling support. *Note:* Always test the bit to ensure that it is the same size as the inlay or insert before actually making the holes in the top ring.

An optional, additional feature for a bowl with top-ring decorations is brass and copper tubing that frames each round or square inlay. Simply purchase the tubing material from a craft, model, or hobby shop. Tubing is usually available in diameters of

¼–½ inch and larger. Prepare a dowel or saw a squared strip to fit the tubing. Cut inlays and metallic pieces into lengths of approximately ¼ inch or as appropriate, and at the angle that closely matches the angle or flair of the bowl's top ring. Glue in combination wood-and-metal inlays with super glues ("Slo-Zip") or similar cyanoacrylate adhesives. This type of adhesive is also available at hobby and model shops.

Once all the pieces are glued in place, make the final bevel cuts with a scroll saw to form the outside and insides of the top ring. Then glue the tubing to the rings, and sand and finish it in the usual manner.

SCALLOPED OR WAVY INSERTS

One basic decorative technique consists of gluing straight pieces of small, thin contrasting strips of wood into the flat-board bowl blank. Once you have cut and assembled the rings, the result will be a sweeping scalloped inlay completely around the bowl. This technique can be used to make very unusual, highly decorative bowls. The results are different on bowls with different top-view shapes.

To make either of the two bowls shown in Illus. 11-7 and 11-8, begin with a walnut blank. This walnut blank will eventually be cut into a 12-sided board, as shown in Illus. 11-10. Cut only four corners off, and glue in strips of maple sized to equal the width of each saw cut (kerf). Once the glue has cured, rotate the blank 30 degrees for the second series of four "cornering" cuts and glued inserts. Finally, make a third set of four cornering cuts, and once again, glue in strips of maple. This will produce the bowl blank as shown in Illus. 11-10.

The bottom foot and the bottom inside of the bowl can be routed out either before or after the strips are glued into the blank. Draw the fluted or round rings of patterns on the blank, and make the bowl in the usual manner.

MULTIPLE-WOOD INSERTS

This technique involves preparing numerous tapered (pie-shaped) inserts of multi-colored woods of various quantities and angles and gluing them together to form a ring (Illus. 11-11 and 11-12). This

Illus. 11-7. A round walnut bowl with a scalloped inlay. Note the straight, untouched top edge.

Illus. 11-8. A modified fluted bowl with inlays that appear to be "draped" over the top edge of the bowl. This bowl was made from the same blank as the round bowl shown in Illus. 11-7. Also note that this bowl has a scalloped top edge, and that the round bowl does not.

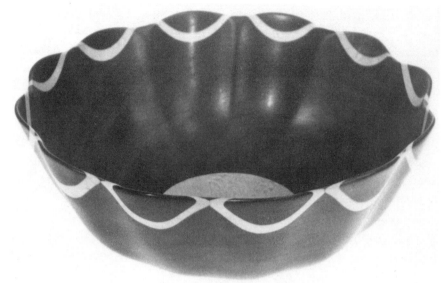

Illus. 11-9. A bottom view of this 12-flute bowl shows the 12 straight pieces used for the top-edge inlays. Note the optional round inlay set into the bottom of the bowl. This inlay was actually used in this case to replace an open knot, thus saving an otherwise good piece of wood.

Illus. 11-10. The bowl blank with 12-sided inlays of ⅛-inch-thick maple.

118

Illus. 11-11. A lobed bowl with a 180-piece inlay sandwiched between two pieces of veneer. This assembly is a special ring located between the top and the second rings of the bowl.

Illus. 11-12. The completed inlay ring for the bowl shown in Illus. 11-11. Note that its inside and outside edges are bevel-sawn to conform to the wall contour created by the bevelled rings that will be glued above and below it.

ring unit alone or used in combination with others is then inserted and glued as a single unit(s) into the bowl during the usual ring-laminating process.

These colorful rings look best when sandwiched between at least two pieces of veneer that contrast with the color of the wood used for the rest of the bowl.

Use the top-view and wall-section full-size patterns to develop a plan to make multiple wood inserts of the size and variety of woods desired. The more pieces used, the smaller and more acute their pie-shaped angles become. Up to a point of practicality,

the more pieces used to make the ring, the more interesting the overall look. Seldom, however, would anyone want to use more than 180 pieces completely around the ring; this would require each wedge-shaped piece to have an included angle of two degrees to complete the 360-degree circle.

A built-up ring inlay composed of 144 pieces of wood does make an attractive decorative feature. To make this type of inlay, you will have to cut each piece to an included angle of 2½ degrees to get a 360-degree ring.

To make either a 144- or 180-piece inlay

119

ring, begin with nine pieces of wood. It's more interesting if all nine pieces are of different species, but fewer species can be used and repeated in whatever makes an appealing pattern. A dark wood is usually placed next to a lighter wood, but this is not a rigid rule. The nine different woods used to make the inlay for the bowl shown in Illus. 11-11 are: mahogany, bloodwood, maple, padauk, cherry, walnut, bubinga, purpleheart, and oak (Illus. 11-12).

Use strips of wood that are ¾ inch thick, 1¼ inches wide, and about 14 inches long. Tilt your table saw to bevel-rip the 2- or 2½-degree angles (as necessary) along one edge for the full length of each piece. See the inset in Illus. 11-13. Make only one rip cut off each piece. However, since you have the material on hand and the saw is set up, you may want to bevel-rip the second side, saving the extra set of bevel-ripped pieces for future use.

To clamp the nine bevel-ripped pieces together, use adjustable hand screws with two plywood pads (cauls) under the jaws to distribute the pressure evenly. You can also make a special clamp from two bevelled pieces of solid wood about 18 inches long. Bevel-rip them to 18 degrees to make the

180-piece inlay, or to 22 degrees to make the 144-piece inlay. Drill a hole in each end of the clamping pieces for a bolt and nut; these will be used to tighten the ends of the assembly. Use a C or hand-screw clamp to apply pressure to the center.

Slip pieces of thin plastic film (sheet) or wax paper in between the nine-piece section and the pressure pads or homemade clamp, to prevent accidentally gluing the section and pads together. Clamp hold-downs across the assembly as well, to prevent the glued pieces from popping out of the pressure pads or homemade clamp.

Once the glue has cured, sand it off the thick edge; then saw ¼-inch-thick slices off the glued assembly (Illus. 11-13). Use the table saw and its mitre gauge setup, with an auxiliary board clamped to the saw, to carry the thin slices safely past the blade. Position a stop block appropriately so that you can cut each slice to exactly the same thickness without measuring the slice.

You will have to cut 20 slices from the glued assembly when making a 180-piece inlay ring, or 16 slices to make a 144-piece inlay ring. Glue the slices (or nine-piece segments) together to form one-half of a circle (Illus. 11-14 and 11-15). Begin by gluing two

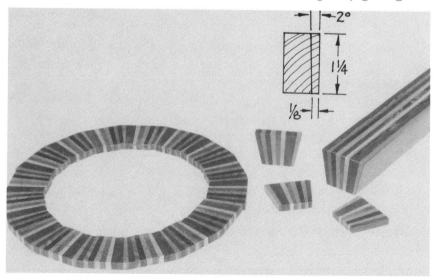

Illus. 11-13. At left: The final nine-piece glued assembly of different woods. Each individual piece has an included angle of 2½ degrees, which makes for a total of 22½ degrees in each assembly of nine pieces. Sixteen end slices ¼-inch thick will complete a full circle for a 144-piece inlay.

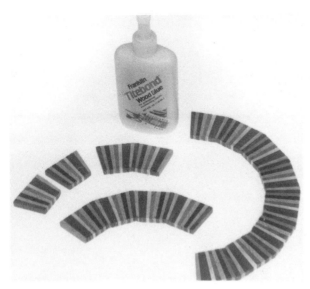

Illus. 11-14. Gluing the nine-piece segments together to make one half of the circular ring, as shown at the right. Note: These segments are not clamped to each other. Just spread glue on them, rub them together, align them with each other, and let the glue set.

Illus. 11-15. One half of an inlay ring. This inlay ring has a checkered design, which is another of many design possibilities. Make any slight corrective fits of the joints to the ends of the half rings (if necessary) before gluing the halves together to form the full rings.

slices together to make a pair, and then gluing the pairs together until half circles are formed. True the mating edges of the two half circles, if necessary, before gluing them together to complete the full circle.

Once the glue in the ring has cured, sand the ring to true it, and level its thickness on the drill press with the ring disc sander.

Next, lay out the ring's top-view profile. Work from the top-view and cross-sectional patterns developed for the bowl.

The usual procedure involved in making a bowl with another ring introduced into the assembly is just slightly different from that just explored. However, it must be thought out carefully at each step. Rout out the bottom and inside as usual, working from top-view and cross-sectional plans. Do not begin cutting the rings until you have made and cut out the new ring (the multiple-piece ring inlay) at the proper bevels and size according to the top-view and cross-sectional patterns.

As you lay the pattern out onto the multiple-wood ring, be sure to extend the registration lines from the pattern. Bevel-cut the outside perimeter of the ring at the appropriate angle (20 degrees for the bowl shown in Illus. 11-11) using the scroll saw. Mark inwards about ¼ inch all around, and bevel-cut the inside of the ring to the same angle.

Now that the multiple-wood ring has been cut out to its top-view shape and has properly bevelled edges, use it as a pattern to lay out the very top ring and the ring that will be directly under it in the assembled bowl. Illus. 11-16 shows this layout being made on the bottom of the bowl blank. Illus. 11-17 shows the layout being made on the top side of the bowl blank for sawing out the second ring, the ring that will be under the multiple wood-inlay ring.

Note: When angle-drilling and bevel-sawing the bowl blank with the bottom side up, make sure you hold the workpiece against the bit and the correct side of the scroll-saw blade during the operation(s), so the direction of the bevel (slant) will be as desired. This is a departure from the usual ring-cutting practice, and can be somewhat confusing. The best approach is to visualize

Illus. 11-16. The inlay ring is sawn out, and is then used to mark lines on the bottom of the bowl blank, as shown, for cutting out the very top ring. Mark around both the inside and outside.

Illus. 11-17. Making the layout on the top side of the bowl blank for sawing out the ring that is right below the top ring. Mark around both the inside and outside of the inlay ring.

what you need to do before drilling the saw-gate hole or making the cut.

Cut two pieces of veneer to glue into the assembly, one above and one below the multiple-wood inlay ring (Illus. 11-18). Cut the veneers approximately ³⁄₁₆ to ¼ inch larger in both the inside and outside directions. When gluing, coat both surfaces of the veneer with glue; this stabilizes the veneer. Be careful when aligning the solid rings and the multiple-wood inlay ring. The veneer makes it difficult to see and line up the registration lines, so inspect the glued-up form from several different positions to ensure that every layer lines up before allowing the glued assembly to set up (Illus. 11-19).

When the glue has cured, sand away the protruding veneer first. Then proceed to sand and shape the walls of the bowl; finally, move on to finish the bowl as usual.

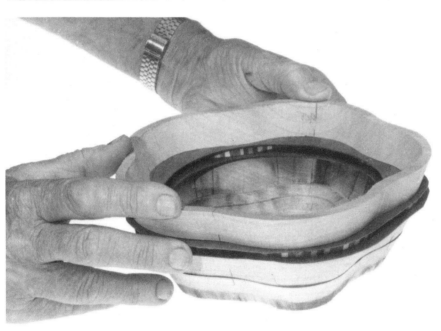

Illus. 11-18. All of the component parts for the 144-piece inlay bowl. Above: The solid wood rings and base. Below: The rough-cut veneers and the multiple-wood inlay ring.

Illus. 11-19. The parts fitted together.

Chapter XII
Undulating Inserts

Probably the most interesting of all bowls are those with wavy, undulating lines of contrasting wood inserts (Illus. 12-1 and 12-2). The lines appear to move up and down as they follow the contour of a modified flute bowl. Bowls with undulating wood inserts are among the most challenging to make, but well worth the effort. Bowls of this type arouse the greatest curiosity, and they motivate everyone (especially woodworkers) to wonder how they were made.

Veneer is the best material to use for the undulating inlays. Any quantity of layers in contrasting colors can be inserted between specially prepared solid wood rings to create the ornamentation desired (Illus. 12-3). One technique that creates an even more charming effect is to make two bowls, each of contrasting woods, at one time, and interchange the parts—preferably just the solid-wood top ring. The bowl shown in Illus. 12-4, for example, is made of walnut. It was

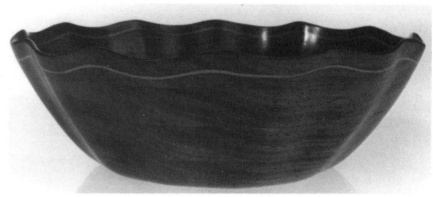

Illus. 12-1. A modified fluted bowl made of padauk, and which has a maple-veneer undulating insert.

Illus. 12-2. A closer look at the undulating line; compare it to the barely visible straight glue line on the top ring, which is indicated by the pencil.

Illus. 12-3. Two bowls with triple-veneer undulating inlays. The bowl on the left is made of beefwood. The bowl on the right is made of maple.

Illus. 12-4. This modified flute bowl, made of walnut, was made at the same time as the solid-maple bowl shown in 12-5. The solid top rings were exchanged to create two stunning bowls. This one has two layers of undulating veneer glued between the rings.

Illus. 12-5.

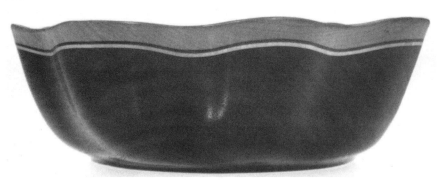

made at the same time as a maple bowl. The solid top rings were exchanged, and two stunning bowls were created.

Undulating inlays can also be made of thicker solid woods, but this process will be examined later because their preparation is more complex than preparing the veneers for the undulating inserts.

The undulating effect is attainable only with bowls of a modified flute design. One reason why is that the undulating effect can

be developed on the side view (Illus. 12-5), because the top-view profile outline of the bowl moves in and out around it. This effect can also be achieved on other types of fluted bowls, although special inclined router cuts have to be made on the surfaces of the rings where they are glued to the undulation inset material (veneer). The more-gentle curves of the modified flute bowl can be routed with a bit that will make that specific type of cut.

A bowl with undulating wood inserts can only be made if two requirements are met. First, the bowl must have a wavy (in and out) top-view outside profile. Second, the inlay or inset(s) glued into the bowl wall must be at an angular or oblique direction to the regular horizontal glue lines common to other bowls made the conventional way. (Study the wall section drawing in Illus. 12-6.) When these two requirements are met, the undulation happens automatically during the course of the bowl's construction.

The ring-cutting procedures normally used to make a bowl are reversed when an undulating inlay bowl is made. These steps follow the usual routing operations of removing the excess material from the inside and bottom areas of the base piece of the bowl.

MODIFIED NINE-FLUTE BOWL WITH AN UNDULATING INLAY

Begin to make this bowl the same way as all bowls, with the routing of the top and bottom of the bowl blank. Make a template from the pattern in Illus. 12-7 for routing the top or inside of the bowl, and complete the routing as you would for other bowls. Rout the bottom of the bowl blank in the usual manner, using a 5¼-inch round template and a 1⁷⁄₁₆-inch compensator, as are used for other bowls. The bowl from this point on will be made from the bottom up (Illus. 12-6). This means that the base section will be sawed out first, and then the third ring will be sawed out.

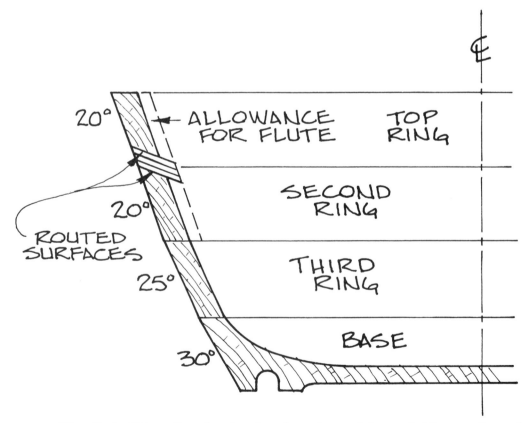

Illus. 12-6. This wall-section drawing shows the special routed oblique surfaces of the top and second rings that have cone-shaped layers of veneer glued between them.

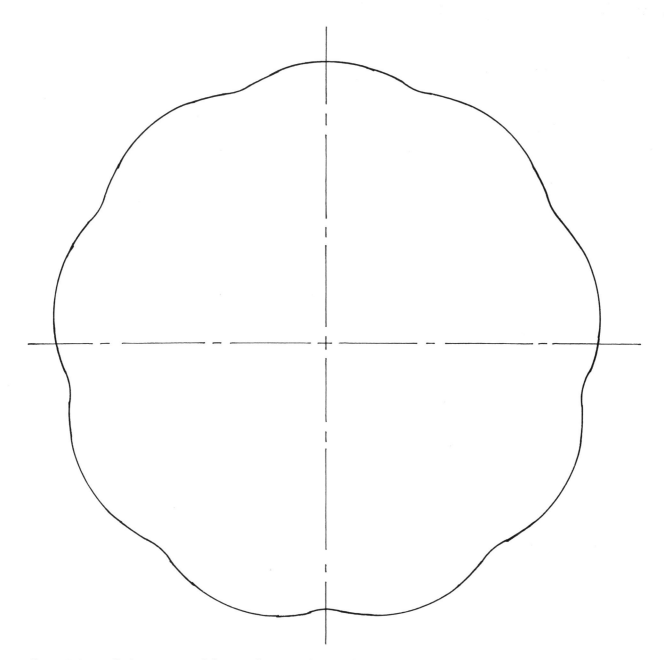

Illus. 12-7. Full-size pattern of the template opening used to rout away the excess material from the top side of the bowl blank.

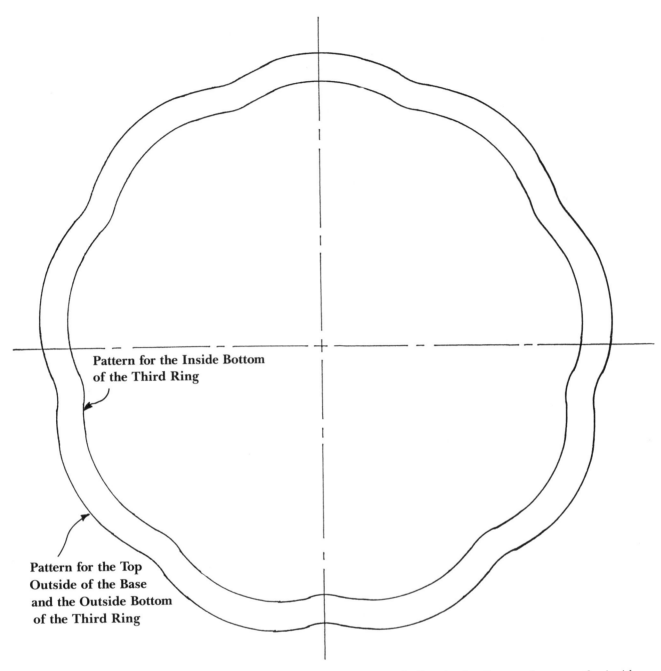

**Pattern for the Inside Bottom
of the Third Ring**

**Pattern for the Top
Outside of the Base
and the Outside Bottom
of the Third Ring**

*Illus. 12-8. Full-size layout pattern lines. The out-
side line, above, is the line used to cut the outside
perimeter of the base. It is also the same line for the
bottom outside surface of the third ring from the top.*

*The inside line is the line used to saw the inside
bottom of the same ring (the third from the top). See
the section drawing, Illus. 12-6.*

Make two patterns from Illus. 12-8 for
drawing around the inside (Illus. 12-9 and
12-10). The bowl blank gives better support
for drawing the lines if made this way. Be

sure to put the register lines on the patterns.
Draw the large pattern on both the top and
bottom of the bowl blank. Draw the small
pattern only on the bottom of the bowl

128

Illus. 12-9. Use a paper pattern to mark the outside bevel cut used to free the base piece of the bowl.

Illus. 12-10. Use the paper patterns to lay out the sawing lines for both the inside and the outside cut of the third ring. Note that this layout is made on the bottom surface of the bowl blank.

Illus. 12-11. Drill the angled hole for the scroll-saw blade from the bottom surface of the bowl blank placed up, as shown here.

blank (12-9 and 12-10).

Drill a hole at 30°; this is used to start the saw blade from the top of the bowl blank where the register line crosses the pattern line. Also drill a hole at 25° from the bottom of the bowl blank at the same point as the top hole. This hole, however, should taper outward as shown in Illus. 12-11. Drill all holes from the bottom of the bowl blank in the same manner.

Saw out the base piece first at a 30-degree bevel. Reset the scroll-saw table to 25 degrees, and cut out the inside of the third ring from the bottom next (the third ring is actually the one next to the base piece). This operation will seem unusual in that the major portion of the bowl blank must be placed on the saw table at the side of the blade *opposite* the side used when the base piece was cut out.

Once the inside of the third ring has been sawn, use the appropriate starting hole and cut out the outside of the third ring from the bottom as shown in Illus. 12-12. At this point in the process, you should have completed sawing out only the base and the ring that will be placed next to it in the built-up, assembled bowl.

Making the Top (First) and Second Rings

Begin by transferring the register lines and the word *top* to the two sawn surfaces of the third ring. Next, place the third ring onto the bottom of the bowl blank with its large diameter down, as shown in Illus. 12-13. Draw around *both* the inside and the outside of the third ring as a pattern to make the sawing layout line for cutting out the second ring (the ring below the top ring).

Adjust the scroll-saw table to 20 degrees and cut out *only* the inside surface (edge) of the second ring, leaving the ring still intact in the blank. Next, cut the oblique or angular gluing surfaces with the router; then cut the ring free from the blank.

Oblique Surface-Routing of the Top and Second Rings

The slanted or inclined gluing surfaces of the bottom of the top (first) ring and the top of the second ring as detailed and shown in the section drawing (Illus. 12-6) are formed

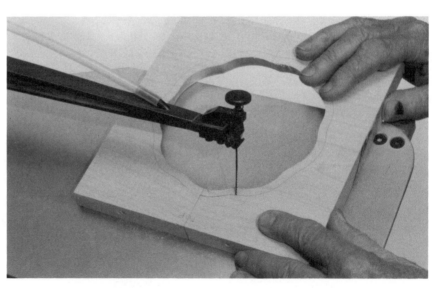

Illus. 12-12. Saw the outside of the third ring with the bottom surface of the bowl blank placed up on the saw, as shown.

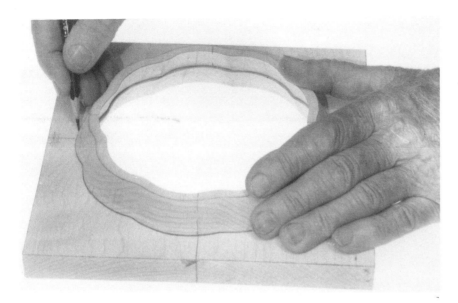

Illus. 12-13. Using the third ring from the top as a pattern, mark the 20-degree cut for the second ring.

with the router. The following are needed for this operation: A Sears No. 9-26465 panel-raising router bit (Illus. 12-16 and 12-18); an auxiliary router base with the integral shop-made extra-large, 1⅞-inch outer-diameter template guide (Illus. 12-15 and Illus. 4-4); and two shop-made hardboard templates with round inside openings (Illus. 12-14).

Make one template with a 7¹⁵⁄₁₆-inch-diameter inside opening. Use it, as shown in Illus. 12-15, to rout the upper oblique gluing surface on the second ring. Make sure that the cross registration lines drawn on the template and on the bowl blank are carefully aligned. Tack the template to two opposite corners of the blank with small headless nails. Complete the routing as shown in Illus. 12-15.

Now, turn the blank over (bottom side

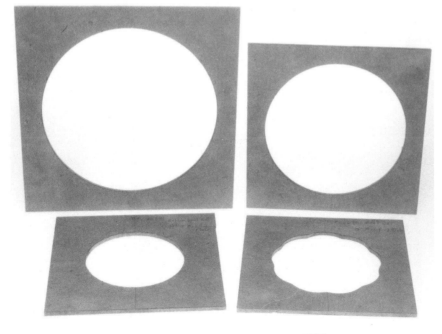

Illus. 12-14. Four routing templates required for making the undulating veneer inlay bowl. The two larger templates shown above are used with a panel-raising bit to form the inclined or slanted gluing surfaces of the first and second rings. The two templates shown below are used to rout the top and bottom surfaces of the base piece.

131

Illus. 12-15. Bowl blank with template attached to rout the top, inclined gluing surface of the second ring. The router shown at the right is set up to make the cut.

up) and proceed to cut the outside of the second ring with the scroll saw, freeing it from the bowl blank. Follow the previously marked line, cutting to a 20-degree bevel. Illus. 12-16 shows the completed second ring. The 20-degree scroll-saw cut made on

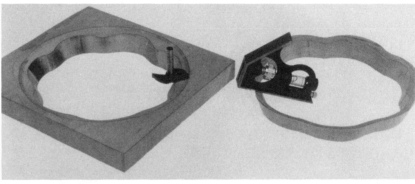

Illus. 12-16. At left is the bowl blank with the template removed. On the right is the cut out second ring, with an inclined gluing surface on its top side.

Illus. 12-17. This large template is attached to the bottom of the bowl blank. Strips of wood the same thickness as the bowl blank itself support the template where it extends beyond the bowl blank. These supports are necessary to maintain a uniform cutting depth completely around the blank.

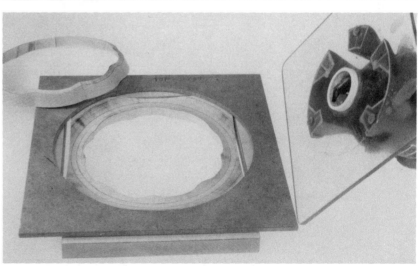

the outside of the second ring also becomes the inside 20-degree sawn surface of the top ring; this surface should remain intact, so do not free it from the bowl blank.

Next, align and attach a ¼-inch-thick hardboard template, with a round inside opening with a 9¹¹⁄₁₆-inch inside-diameter, to the *bottom* side of the bowl blank. This setup is used as before, but the inclined gluing surface should be routed completely around what will be the bottom gluing surface of the top ring.

Illus. 12-17 shows a completed top ring, and the template and router setup to make its inclined gluing surface before it is sawn free from the blank (Illus. 12-18). Illus. 12-19 shows the outside edge of the top ring being laid out; the second ring is being used as a pattern so the final ring can be bevel-sawn to its required 20-degree angle and simultaneously freed from the blank (Illus. 12-20 and 12-21). Remember to transfer the register lines and the word *top* to the sawn surfaces of the rings.

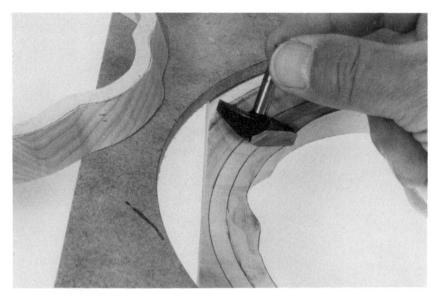

Illus. 12-18. A closeup look at the routing necessary with a panel-raising bit to make the inclined gluing surfaces of the top ring (shown here) and the second ring.

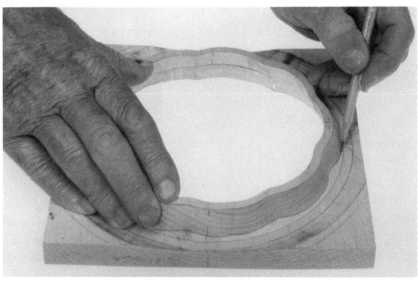

Illus. 12-19. Laying out the top ring, using the second ring as a pattern. The inclined surfaces of both rings are mated.

Illus. 12-20. Making the last cut on the top ring at 20 degrees.

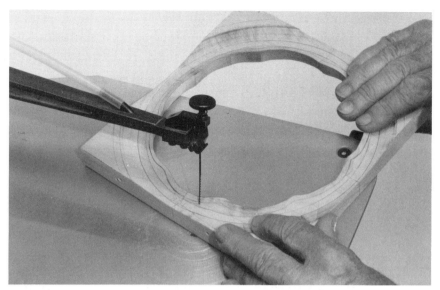

Illus. 12-21. The top ring shown on the right was cut from the bowl blank shown on the left. Note the inclined gluing surface on its bottom.

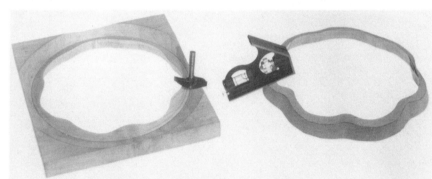

Preparing the Veneer Inserts

The inclined gluing surfaces around the top and second rings will not match flat veneer. The veneer has to be formed to a slight cone shape. This can be easily done by cutting four individual circular segments from a sheet of veneer with their edges butt-glued together (Illus. 12-22). Illus. 12-23 gives the dimensions needed to make a veneer-cutting pattern or template.

The ends of the veneer segments should be glued as shown in Illus. 12-22. When they are glued according to the plan, you will avoid severe contrasts of color at the veneer butt joints. Glue together all darker edges and all lighter edges of the veneer if there are color variations across the width of the veneer sheet being used.

Illus. 12-24 and 12-25 show how to glue the thin butt ends of the veneer segments to

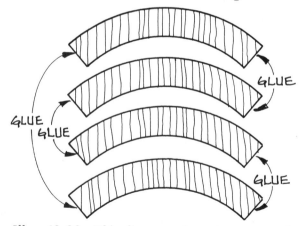

Illus. 12-22. This diagram shows how to get the correct grain direction, and how to edge-glue the veneer pieces to achieve uniform coloring around the bowl when the pieces are glued together at their ends.

134

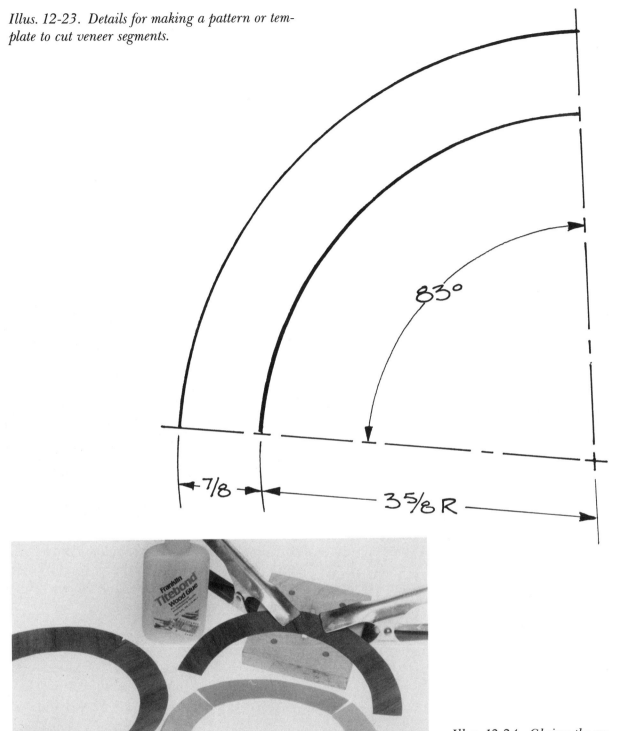

Illus. 12-23. Details for making a pattern or template to cut veneer segments.

83°

7/8

3 5/8 R

Illus. 12-24. Gluing the veneer sections together. Note that the joint is over an opening cut into a supporting block, and is being held there with spring clamps.

135

Illus. 12-25. The conical veneer(s) conforms to the inclined gluing surfaces of the solid wood rings.

each other. Use a quick-setting adhesive or yellow carpenter's glue. When four segments are glued together, the flexible veneer takes on a conical shape that conforms to the inclined gluing surfaces around the top and second rings (Illus. 12-26).

The glue-up preparation procedures for this bowl(s) are essentially the same as those used to make other bowls. The flat, horizontal gluing surfaces located between the base piece and the third ring and between the second and third rings are sanded in the usual way, with the ring disc sander on the drill press.

The oblique, router-cut gluing surfaces between the top and second rings do not require any gluing preparation. When gluing, make sure that all the layers are orientated with the registration lines, and that the words *top* on each layer are aligned with each other; this ensures the least-conspicuous grain-pattern arrangement.

When the bowl has been glued, sand away the excess veneer inlays with coarse sandpaper, so that the veneer conforms to the surrounding surfaces of the bowl. Now the scalloped or wavy undulating line(s) will stand out! Two final suggestions: First, thin the top edge. Second, scallop completely around the top edge, so that it corresponds to the line of the undulating veneer insert around the bowl.

Illus. 12-26. At left is a conical veneer inlay. At right a conical veneer inlay has been inserted between the solid rings.

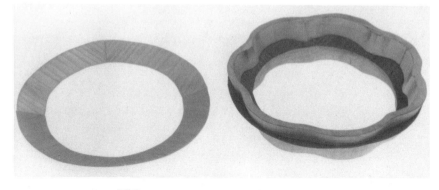

DOUBLE UNDULATING INSERTS OF SOLID WOOD

Bowls with double undulating inserts of solid wood are more challenging in that the oblique glue lines have to match those of the inlay (Illus. 12-27 and 12-28). Otherwise, the bowl is made in exactly the same manner as the undulating veneer inlay bowl previously described, except for the following two differences: First, the insert or inlay piece is made from a separate piece of solid wood inlay that is made so that its two oblique gluing surfaces slant in opposite directions (Illus. 12-28). Second, the gluing surface on the top edge of the second ring is inclined in the opposite direction as the cut made for the same ring of a veneer inlaid undulating bowl.

The inclined gluing surfaces of the inlay are routed from both the top and bottom sides of the separate board blank, as shown in Illus. 12-30. Appropriately sized templates must be made to correspond to the desired sizes (diameters) required. This is also true for the routing of the inclined gluing surfaces of the second and top rings.

Illus. 12-31 shows the routing arrangement when the inclined gluing surfaces for the top and second ring are being made. Note that the inclined surface of the second ring is routed from the top side of the bowl blank after the edges of the base and the third ring are bevel-sawn and removed from the blank.

The inclined surface of the top ring is routed from the bottom side after the sec-

Illus. 12-27. A beautiful walnut bowl with a double-edged undulating inlay of solid maple.

Illus. 12-28. This view of the same bowl clearly shows the dramatic effect of the double-edge undulating inlay.

137

*Illus. 12-29. This section draw-
ing shows the opposing inclined
gluing surfaces of the solid-wood
inlay insert.*

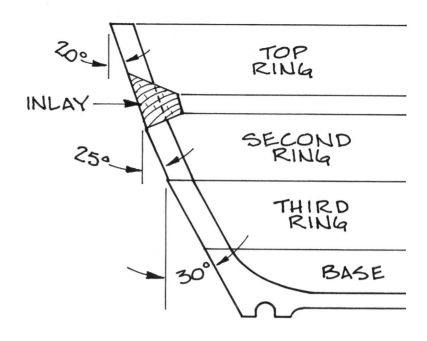

*Illus. 12-30. Routing the inclined
gluing surfaces of the inlay that
will be cut free from the board
blank with a scroll saw. This inlay
is made from a separate blank.*

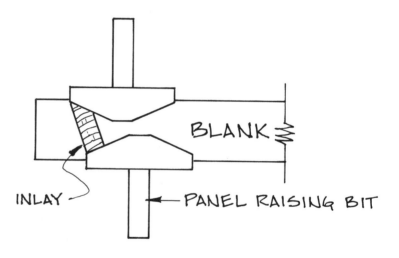

*Illus. 12-31. Arrangement for
routing the inclined gluing surfaces of the top and second rings
with a Sears panel-raising bit.
Rout the gluing surface of the second ring from the top side of the
bowl blank after sawing the base
and third ring free from the blank.
Rout the top ring's gluing surface
from the bottom side of the blank
after routing the second ring and
cutting it free from the bowl blank.*

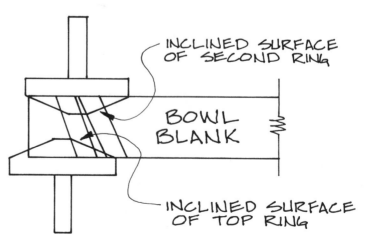

138

ond ring is routed and cut from the blank with a scroll saw (Illus. 12-31).

Making the double undulating inlay bowl is a challenge to one's overall designing skills and ability to execute cutting procedures. You must pick out the top-view design you prefer, make the pattern and cross-sectional plan, and then design and make the appropriately sized routing templates. The resulting bowl will be, however, distinctly different in design, and will evoke words of admiration.

Chapter XIII
Miscellaneous Bowl-Making
Techniques

The bowl-making techniques described in previous chapters can be expanded on, altered slightly, or used in combinations to create unusual-looking bowls. These approaches to bowl-making are described and illustrated in this chapter.

FLUTED BULBOUS BOWLS

Fluted bulbous bowls are spectacular-looking bowls that need just slightly more planning and construction (Illus. 13-1 and 13-2). They look as if they were hand-carved from one massive piece of wood. These bowls are actually made as if they are two bowls, one inverted over the other.

Rather than begin with two individual board blanks, it's best to begin with a blank that is 2 inches thick. Draw registration lines on the blank to keep the grain orientation; then resaw its thickness so that you have two bowl blanks. Make the top half of the bowl from the upper piece, and the bottom part of the bowl from the other piece.

Somewhat similar processes are employed to make the dry-flower vases shown in Illus. 13-3. You can rout away the inside

areas of vertical laminations, using this technique with or without sawn rings, to create interesting vessels.

MULTIPLE-PIECE BOWL BLANKS

One way to create some striking and bold-looking bowls is to make them from blanks that consist of a glued-up assembly of wood pieces of different colors, sizes and shapes. Bowl blanks can be made of alternately

Illus. 13-1. A fluted, bulbous bowl made of black walnut.

140

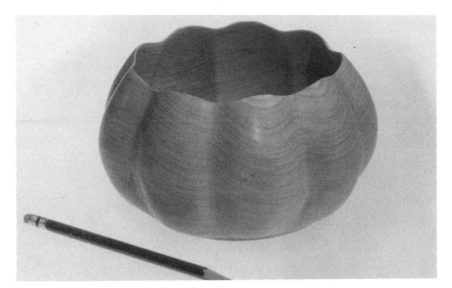

Illus. 13-2. A cherry bulbous bowl.

Illus. 13-3. Two dry-flower vases. The vase on the left is made of silky oak. The vase on the right is made of bubinga. The left vase has one sawn piece at its center (like a sawn ring), the two layers on each side of the piece were routed out before assembly. The vase on the right simply consists of two pieces that were routed on their insides before being glued together.

laminated strips, pie-shaped pieces, or any shape that can be created. Carefully control the patterns and grain orientations with the aid of the registration lines. You will be surprised what designs can be created from the blank once the rings are sawn free from the blank and stacked together. Several examples are given below.

Square-Oval Bowl

The square-oval bowl shown in Illus. 13-4 is made of maple and bloodwood. A piece consisting of five strips of bloodwood and six strips of maple was glued up first. Four pieces were cut off the end, and one piece was diagonally cut to make the two angular corner pieces. All the pieces were assembled and glued together to form the bowl blank shown in Illus. 13-5. Then the bowl was made in the usual manner.

Bowl with Pie-Shaped Pieces

A bowl like the one shown in Illus. 13-6 can be created by assembling pie-shaped pieces

141

into a round bowl blank. The wood for this particular bowl was selected for its grain so that as the bowl rings were sawn, their cut surfaces produced a quarter-sawn effect completely around the bowl.

Illus. 13-4. This square-oval bowl is three inches deep and has a full-flair top edge. This bowl is eight inches across, and is made from alternating strips of ¼-inch-thick (wide) bloodwood and maple.

Illus. 13-5. The half-size pattern for the bowl blank that makes the bowl shown in Illus. 13-4.

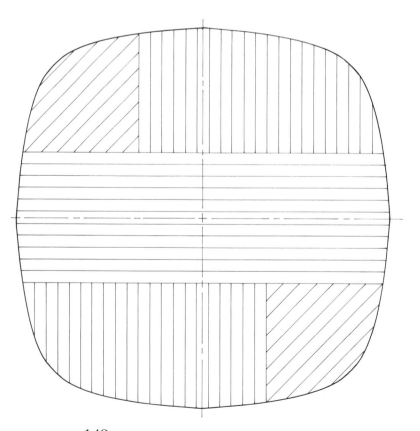

Elongated Bowl

Illus. 13-7 shows an elongated bowl made essentially the same way as the bowl shown in Illus. 13-6, but with a straight piece glued across the middle. Six pie-shaped pieces, cut at thirty degrees, make up each end of this bowl blank. A scroll saw was used to trim the top edge of the bowl to an irregular shape after the bowl was assembled.

SLICED AND REGLUED BOWLS

This process involves taking a fully assembled bowl and cutting it into segments or pieces of various configurations with a band saw. These pieces can then be reglued, with veneers inserted to take up the space removed by the band-saw cut. Another ap-

Illus. 13-6. This 10-inch-diameter oak bowl consists of 30 pie-shaped pieces, each cut to 12 degrees.

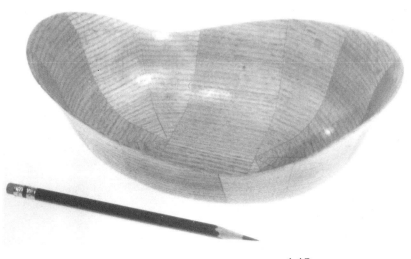

Illus. 13-7. This oak bowl also has an irregular, wavy top edge that was cut after the bowl was assembled.

143

proach is to interchange pieces if you are making identical types of bowls of different woods at the same time. Examples of techniques involving slicing and regluing bowls are given below.

Interlocking Rings on Bulbous Bowl

The bowl shown in Illus. 13-8 is made by cutting uniform, straight-line slices off the outside of a round, assembled bowl, and

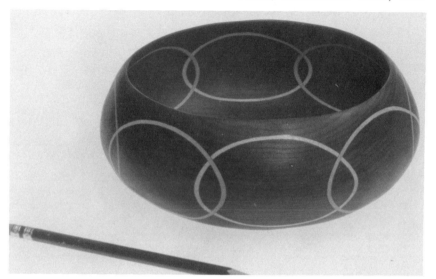

Illus. 13-8. A bulbous walnut bowl with interlocking ring inlays.

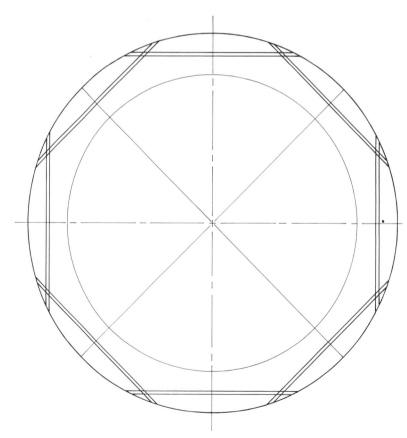

Illus. 13-9. A half-size top-view pattern and wall section for making a bowl that appears to have a pattern of interlocking rings spaced uniformly around it.

144

then regluing these parts and inserting pieces of maple veneer between them. You must, however, make a jig that will be guided by a clamped straightedge or the fence or mitre slot on your band saw. This cutting jig should be eight-sided or made to index properly, so that every slicing cut will be identical to the others. First, cut one set of four opposite cuts. After the pieces are glued back in place, with the veneer inserts between them, make the second set of four slicing cuts. Illus. 13-9 gives the half-size top-view pattern for the bowl.

Angular Veneer Inlays

You can also create a bowl with angular veneer inlays by cutting an assembled bowl into various pieces with a band saw, and then gluing the veneer into the saw kerf space (Illus. 13-10 and 13-11). To make the diagonal- and angular-line inlays for this bowl, you must saw it in an upright rather than a horizontal position, as done with the interlocking ring design.

The band-sawing operation is shown in Illus. 13-12. The details of the components used to make the jig are given in Illus. 13-13. Note in the illustrations that a "three-point" mounting block is temporarily spot-glued with super glue to the bottom of the bowl outside the foot. This mounting block has a threaded insert which is used to hold it, along with the attached bowl, to an angular support block on the jig. Three successive cuts are made with the bowl held at 20 degrees to the blade. After each cut, a piece of veneer is inserted and allowed to set be-

Illus. 13-10. This modified-flute bowl, made of purpleheart wood, has diagonal veneer inlays.

Illus. 13-11. Another view of the same bowl.

Illus. 13-12. A glued-up bowl is band-sawn into oblique segments with the aid of this jig. After one cut is completed and the veneer is inserted and glued, the bowl is rotated 120 degrees, and then cut and glued again. This sequence is repeated a third time.

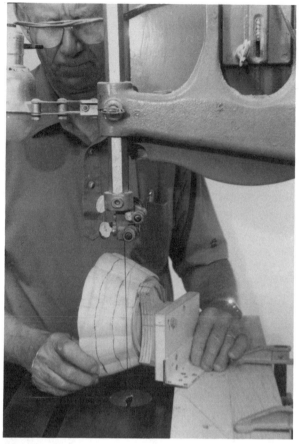

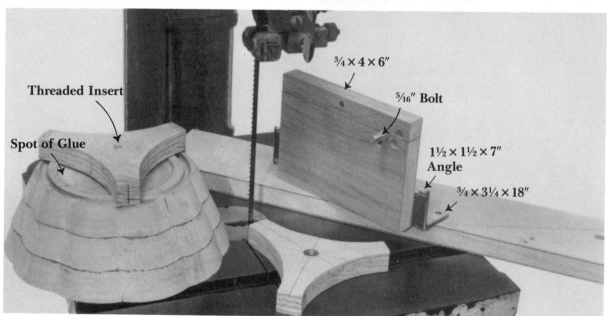

Threaded Insert

Spot of Glue

¾ × 4 × 6″

⁵⁄₁₆″ Bolt

1½ × 1½ × 7″
Angle

¾ × 3¼ × 18″

Illus. 13-13. Details for making a band-saw bowl-holding jig. Note the three-point mounting blocks (on the table and glued to the bowl) with a threaded insert in their centers. Only one block is actually necessary.

Illus. 13-14. A "patchwork" bowl that consists of three different woods: maple, cherry, and walnut.

Illus. 13-15. A patchwork bowl with a scalloped top edge.

fore the bowl is rotated one-third of a full turn and cut again. When the band-sawing operations are complete, the bowl is carefully removed with a sharp chisel.

"Patchwork" Bowls

"Patchwork" bowls are obliquely segmented bowls band-sawn in the same way as the previously described bowls, with one difference. Three separate bowls are assembled, each of a different kind of wood, and then sawn into identical parts. Then their pieces are interchanged and glued into each new bowl. The bowl shown in Illus. 13-14 was made from parts of three bowls made of cherry, walnut, and maple.

Patchwork or three-wood bowls are best made from bowls that are symmetrical in shape. Make sure that the glue lines are properly aligned. These bowls look best when their top and bottom pieces have the same kind of wood.

NOVELTY BOWLS

"Novelty" bowls are those bowls made with a combination of different techniques. The bowl shown in Illus. 13-16 has a bold, wavy inlay that results from a specially inlaid bowl blank (Illus. 13-17). The inlay goes through the full thickness ($^{25}/_{32}$ inch) of the bowl blank. Any top-view bowl shape can be used, but bowls with odd-numbered lobes produce the most interesting results.

Illus. 13-18 shows another way to prepare a two-color blank that will produce a bowl that will look very similar to the one shown in Illus. 13-16. Each design variation in the blank will yield somewhat different results.

Illus. 13-16. A "novelty" bowl that appears to have a bold, wavy inlay. This five-lobed bowl is made of limba, and has a padauk inlay.

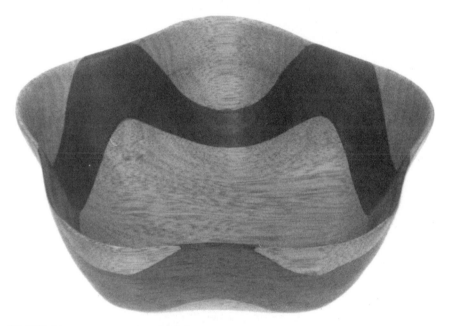

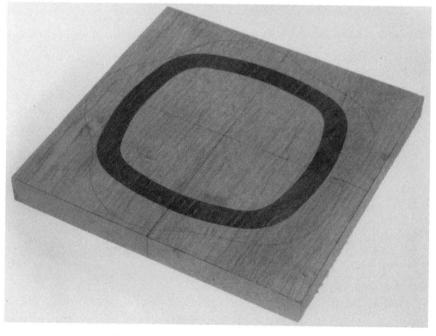

Illus. 13-17. The bowl shown in Illus. 13-16 was made from this blank. The dark, rounded-square inlay is made of padauk. It goes completely through the bowl blank. The surrounding wood is limba.

148

Illus. 13-18. An alternate way to work up a blank for making bowls that will be very similar to the one shown in Illus. 13-16.

REDUCING AND ENLARGING BOWL DESIGNS

Bowl designs can also be enlarged and reduced to accommodate any specific need or personal preferences. Illus. 13-19 shows a very large salad bowl. Simply enlarge or reduce the top-view and sectional plans given in Chapter II accordingly. It will be extremely helpful if you use a good copy machine—that is, one that can reduce and enlarge in increments of one percent.

Illus. 13-19. This very large salad bowl has a diameter of 12 inches. It is made of three layers of 1¾-inch-thick cherry that have been glued together with waterproof glue.

USING DIFFERENT MATERIALS

You can also create unusual-looking bowls by experimenting with a wide range of materials, including Baltic birch plywoods, and various plastics such as the hard surfacing materials used for countertops and liquid plastics used for special inlaying. The possibilities are endless for those who want to challenge their creative instincts.

Chapter XIV
Glues and Finishes

The information presented in this chapter is directed towards those woodworkers inexperienced in gluing and finishing. It is meant to be used as a guideline. Today, the market is flooded with numerous kinds of glues and finishes. Most woodworkers experiment with these different products until they find those that satisfy their particular needs. It is impossible to describe in detail all of the product possibilities, so a general analysis of certain types is given.

GLUES

White and Yellow Glues

The popular white and yellow glues used for furniture-making and general woodworking are *not* recommended for critical joints in bowl-making. Although these glues can form a strong bond on mating surfaces, the surfaces have a tendency to creep with changes in atmospheric humidity. This can be detected by looking at the finish and by feeling the joints of the thin bowl walls, which will develop slight ripples. White and yellow glues are best used for general utility work, such as when fabricating jigs and fixtures for bowl-making.

Plastic Resin Glue

Plastic resin glue is an ideal glue for both novice and professional bowl makers (Illus. 14-1). It comes as a powder, and is simply mixed with water. Plastic resin glue is not waterproof, but it is highly and sufficiently moisture-resistant when cured. Before it cures, it can be cleaned up with soap and water.

Illus. 14-1. Plastic resin glue is easy to use. It mixes and can be cleaned up with water, and it is ideal for bonding the bowl ring laminations.

Once set, this glue is not easily removed from wood, tools, or fabrics, so employ the necessary precautions. It is best mixed in plastic containers because it does not adhere to plastics. Plastic resin glue is not a gap-filling glue, so the joints must be well prepared and must fit tightly together without any openings.

Epoxy Glues

Though epoxy glues are messy and generally more difficult to use than plastic resin glues, they have distinct advantages. In addition to being waterproof, epoxy is the best type of glue to use for bonding oily and acidic woods or dissimilar materials. Use epoxy for gluing teakwood and cocobolo.

Epoxy is a gap-filling glue and good to use if one must glue joints with visible, open spaces. The resulting glue lines are always clear. Disadvantages to using epoxies are that they must be cleaned up with toxic solvents, and that some plastic resins are toxic until properly cured.

Resorcinol Glues

A resorcinol glue is a liquid resin that comes with a powdered catalyst. Although resorcinol is also a very tough, durable, and waterproof glue, it should as a rule be avoided for bowl-making. Its major disadvantage is that resorcinol glue lines are highly visible and appear distinctively red-purple. With most woods, this is distracting and totally unacceptable, unless you want to visually accentuate glue lines.

There are many types of other adhesives available that may or may not be satisfactory. Be wary of those that have a short "shelf life." If a glue with a shelf life is not used within the designated time, it will not work. Some glues must be used within as little as 30 days.

FINISHES

Adding a finish to the bowl is an important step. The quality of the finish is one measure of the bowl-maker's craftsmanship. A well-finished bowl is one that feels and looks good.

There are numerous brands and types of finishes that are suitable for decorative bowls (Illus. 14-2). Almost any one of these finishes will work to some extent, but as with any other specific woodworking activity, certain kinds are more effective. Clear finishes, for example, will accentuate the beautiful natural wood colors.

When using any type of finish, pay attention to the following guidelines: Use the finish in a well-ventilated area. It should also be used at the proper room temperature and in the proper environment. Many finishes require a room temperature of at least 70 degrees Fahrenheit and dust-free conditions. Also, make sure that you properly dispose of all solvents and rags, to prevent spontaneous combustion and other hazards. Finally, whenever using a new finish for the first time, always test it on scrap wood. The results may be extremely different than expected.

Following is a description of the advantages and disadvantages of certain types of finishes.

Epoxy Finishes

Harry Nohr, a former, well-known turner from Mineral Point, Wisconsin, produced bowls that became popular not only because they were beautiful, but also because of the finish that he used on them. This finish was a type of epoxy that was acceptable for food contact according to the United States Department of Agriculture. The Nohr epoxy finish is still available from

152

Peterson Chemical Corp., P.O. Box 102, Sheboygan Falls, Wisconsin 53085.

Epoxy finishes are tough, durable, and, once cured, safe for use with food. They do have disadvantages, however. They are difficult to apply evenly and, like lacquers, are best sprayed on for uniformity. When they are used on the irregular walls of unturned bowls, they will be difficult to apply and rub out.

Oil Finishes

An oil finish may be the best type of finish to use in that it beautifies a bowl, can be easily applied, and is durable. Once cured, most oil finishes can safely come in contact with food, but be sure to check with the manufacturer.

Several different types of oil finishes are available today. Tung and linseed oil are two of the basic oils used in combination with any one or more of various types of resins.

Some oil finishes have greater resin-to-oil ratios than other. Consequently, bowls with these finishes will have dull, semi-gloss, or glossy surfaces. More applications of the resin will produce a higher gloss. Determining whether to add a dull, semi-gloss, or glossy surface to a bowl is a matter of individual preference.

One distinct advantage of most oil finishes is that they penetrate the wood. Oil finishes toughen the fibre of the wood and harden it, and show less overall wear than top-coat finishes such as lacquer, polyurethane, and varnish.

There is one oil finish available that is marketed specifically as a bowl finish. It is called Behlen's Salad Bowl Oil Finish. This finish is approved by the Food and Drug Administration for use in contact with food. It is available in most woodworking supply stores and mail-order catalogues. Behlen's Salad Bowl Oil Finish is a ready-to-use finish and, as with most oil finishes, is easier to use when it is wiped on.

Minwax® Antique Oil Finish is another effective oil finish (Illus. 14-2). Bowls with five to seven coats of Minwax look as good today as when made five years ago.

Using Oil Finishes

Sanding

In order to get an effective finish on the bowl, you have to first sand the wood. This process should involve no fewer than three

Illus. 14-2. To determine the specific finish to use on a wood bowl, you will have to pick the one that best meets the service requirements for the bowl's use and imparts the "look" you want for the bowl.

153

progressively finer grits of abrasives. It is essential that you completely sand away all deep scratches before moving on to a finer-grit abrasive. This also involves removing the scratches left by the previous, coarser sandpaper. Progressing from 120- to 240- and finally to 320-grit abrasives will produce a smooth bowl.

Look the bowl over carefully, to ensure that all the scratches have been removed. If you do not remove the scratch, it will become very evident when the first coat of finish is applied. If you discover such scratches after the first coat is applied, simply sand away the finish and the scratches. When using oil finishes, you can generally remove the scratched area only without having to worry that lap marks will appear when the finish is reapplied.

Applying Oil Finishes

The best way to apply oil finishes is with a rag. Wear plastic or rubber gloves. Pour a small amount of finish into the bowl and spread it over the inside and outside surfaces of the bowl (Illus. 14-3). Keep the surfaces well wetted for approximately 15 to 20 minutes, allowing the first application to soak in. On wood with side grain, you may reach a point where the wood will not absorb any more finish at this time.

While they are wet, sand the surfaces with 500- or 600-grit wet/dry abrasive. The fine wood removed will become deposited in the pores to produce a beautiful, smooth surface. Recoat with additional oil to maintain a wet surface for sanding. Wipe away the excess finish with paper towels or rags to dry off the surfaces.

After 24 hours, apply another coat. Repeat this as many times as you feel necessary or to achieve the quality of finish desired. Once the final coat has set for 24 hours, hand-rub the bowl with 0000 steel wool. This will smooth the surfaces and remove any excess oil that may have leached out of the pores.

Water-Based Finishes

The new water-based finishes are rapidly replacing many of the conventional furniture and cabinetry lacquer and polyurethane finishes. Current research supports their use. Obviously, if for no other reasons than safety and environmental concerns, these new finishes warrant further testing and consideration.

Illus. 14-3. A penetrating oil finish looks more natural than a glossy surface finish such as lacquer and polyurethane.

154

Metric Equivalents

INCHES TO MILLIMETRES AND CENTIMETRES

MM—millimetres   *CM—centimetres*

Inches	MM	CM	Inches	CM	Inches	CM
⅛	3	0.3	9	22.9	30	76.2
¼	6	0.6	10	25.4	31	78.7
⅜	10	1.0	11	27.9	32	81.3
½	13	1.3	12	30.5	33	83.8
⅝	16	1.6	13	33.0	34	86.4
¾	19	1.9	14	35.6	35	88.9
⅞	22	2.2	15	38.1	36	91.4
1	25	2.5	16	40.6	37	94.0
1¼	32	3.2	17	43.2	38	96.5
1½	38	3.8	18	45.7	39	99.1
1¾	44	4.4	19	48.3	40	101.6
2	51	5.1	20	50.8	41	104.1
2½	64	6.4	21	53.3	42	106.7
2	76	7.6	22	55.9	43	109.2
3½	89	8.9	23	58.4	44	111.8
4	102	10.2	24	61.0	45	114.3
4½	114	11.4	25	63.5	46	116.8
5	127	12.7	26	66.0	47	119.4
6	152	15.2	27	68.6	48	121.9
7	178	17.8	28	71.1	49	124.5
8	203	20.3	29	73.7	50	127.0

ABOUT THE AUTHORS

Patrick Spielman's love of wood began when, as a child, he transformed fruit crates into toys. Now this prolific and innovative woodworker is respected worldwide as a teacher and author.

His most famous contribution to the woodworking field has been his perfection of a method to season green wood with polyethylene glycol 1000 (PEG). He went on to invent, manufacture, and distribute the PEG-Thermovat chemical seasoning system.

During his many years as shop instructor in Wisconsin, Spielman published manuals, teaching guides, and more than 14 popular books, including *Modern Wood Technology*, a college text. He also wrote six educational series on wood technology, tool use, processing techniques, design, and wood-product planning.

Author of the best-selling *Router Handbook*, Spielman has served as editorial consultant to a professional magazine, and his products, techniques, and many books have been featured in numerous periodicals.

This pioneer of new ideas and inventor of countless jigs, fixtures, and designs used throughout the world is a unique combination of expert woodworker and brilliant teacher—all of which endear him to his many readers and to his publisher.

At Spielmans Wood Works in the woods of northern Door County, Wisconsin, he and his family create and sell some of the most durable and popular furniture products and designs available.

Carl L. Roehl is an accomplished "do-it-yourselfer" who began working with wood at an early age. Included among the many items he has built are midget auto racers, hang gliders, a sports car, shop equipment for his workshop, and even his own home. His system of decorative bowl-making is the result of almost a decade of research and trial and error.

Should you wish to write Pat or Carl, please forward your letters to Sterling Publishing Company.

Charles Nurnberg
Sterling Publishing Company

Current Books by Patrick Spielman

Alphabets and Designs for
 Wood Signs
 (and Sherry Spielman)

Carving Large Birds
 (and Bill Dehos)

Carving Wild Animals: Life-Size
 Figures
 (and Bill Dehos)

Classic Fretwork Scroll Saw Patterns
 (and James Reidle)

Gluing and Clamping

Making Country-Rustic
 Wood Projects
 (and Sherry Spielman Valitchka)

Making Wood Decoys

Making Wood Signs

Realistic Decoys
 (and Keith Bridenhagen)

Router Basics

Router Handbook

Router Jigs & Techniques

Scroll Saw Basics

Scroll Saw Country Patterns
 (and Sherry Spielman Valitchka)

Scroll Saw Handbook

Scroll Saw Fretwork Patterns
 (and James Reidle)

Scroll Saw Fretwork Techniques and
 Projects
 (and James Reidle)

Scroll Saw Pattern Book
 (and Patricia Spielman)

Scroll Saw Puzzle Patterns
 (and Patricia Spielman)

Sharpening Basics

Spielman's Original Scroll Saw
 Patterns
 (and Patricia Spielman)

Victorian Scroll Saw Patterns

Working Green Wood with PEG

Index